D1712377

# ORIGINAL NARRATIVE

OF THE

# BOSTON MASSACRE.

BOSTON MASSACRE, MARCH 5, 1770.

A SHORT

# NARRATIVE

OF THE

# HORRID MASSACRE IN BOSTON,

PERPETRATED IN THE

## EVENING OF THE FIFTH DAY OF MARCH, 1770,

BY

## SOLDIERS OF THE 29th REGIMENT,

WHICH

WITH THE 14TH REGIMENT WERE THEN QUARTERED THERE;

WITH SOME

OBSERVATIONS ON THE STATE OF THINGS PRIOR
TO THAT CATASTROPHE.

Originally printed by order of the Town of Boston, 1770.

Re-published 1849 with notes and illustrations
by John Doggett, Jr.

**BOOKS FOR LIBRARIES PRESS**

**FREEPORT, NEW YORK**

First Published 1849
Reprinted 1971

E215.4
B756

INTERNATIONAL STANDARD BOOK NUMBER:
0-8369-5683-4


LIBRARY OF CONGRESS CATALOG CARD NUMBER:
71-150170


PRINTED IN THE UNITED STATES OF AMERICA

# NOTE
## (To The Edition of 1849)

———•———

THE following pages contain the original official account of the
BOSTON MASSACRE of the 5th of March, 1770. It was drawn up
by a committee appointed by the town, consisting of the Honorable
JAMES BOWDOIN, Dr. JOSEPH WARREN, and SAMUEL PEMBERTON, Esq.
The report was submitted to a town meeting held at Faneuil Hall, by
adjournment, on the 19th of March, and was ordered to be printed.
It was intended principally for circulation in England, and a vessel
was chartered by the town to take out copies to London. To the
copies circulated in America, were added a Circular Letter, addressed
by the Committee to the Duke of Richmond, and other distinguished
personages in England.

The frontispiece representing the massacre, is a fac-simile of an
original engraving in the library of the New York Historical Society,
engraved and published in Boston immediately after the event, by
PAUL REVERE. It is supposed to give a somewhat exaggerated
idea, however, of the scene it purports to represent. The sign of
"Butcher's Hall," affixed to the custom-house, is, of course, a fancy
title.

The plan of the town of Boston, copied from one published in the
"Gentleman's and London Magazine," for 1774, may be useful to
those unacquainted with the changes in the streets, their names, &c.,
since that period.

The present edition, with the exception of the subjoined "Additional Observations," which are obtained from a copy of this work in
the library of Harvard College, is an exact reprint from an original
in the library of the New York Historical Society, containing the full
appendix, certificates, and circular of the Committee. To which is
prefixed an account of the events of the few days preceding the massacre, drawn up by the late Hon. ALDEN BRADFORD ; and the Report

made by JOHN HANCOCK, SAMUEL ADAMS, JOSEPH WARREN, and others, presented at the meeting of the citizens on the 12th of March. The whole presenting, it is believed, the most complete and authentic account which has been published of the massacre.

Such additional explanatory notes as have been deemed necessary for the convenience of the reader, are distinguished from the original notes by the initial—D.

# EVENTS

## FEW DAYS PRECEDING THE MASSACRE.

[*From Bradford's History of Massachusetts.*]

---

THE conduct of the citizens of Boston, notwithstanding some state-
ments of a different import, it is believed, may be well vindicated
from the charge of having rashly occasioned the awful catastrophe
of the 5th of March, 1770. It is true, that the minds of the people
were greatly irritated, and that some individuals were abusive in their
language towards the military. But whenever examination was carefully made, it appeared that the soldiers were the first to assault, to
threaten, and to apply contemptuous epithets to the inhabitants.

Every circumstance connected with this wanton and sanguinary
event is important to be noticed. The people were provoked be-
yond endurance; and they can be justly accused only of resisting a
fierce and vindictive soldiery, at the hazard of life. On the 22d of
February, a few boys appeared in one of the streets, bearing some
coarse paper paintings, with the figures of the importers of British
goods. They were met by one R——, who was known to be an in-
former to the custom-house officers, against the citizens suspected of
attempts to evade the laws. He endeavored to prevail with a coun-
tryman, then passing, to destroy the pageantry. But the man declined; and he attempted himself to mutilate and deface them. This
occasioned a collection of people who were in the vicinity of the spot.
R—— was very abusive in his language, and charged some of the
citizens who had assembled, with perjury, and threatened to prose-
cute them. But they seemed to have considered him too insignificant
to be noticed. The boys, however, who were quite young, and who
had brought the pictures into the street, followed the man to his
house, and gave him some opprobrious and reproachful language,
which were the only means of redress in their power, for his attack.
The moment he entered his dwelling, he seized a gun; this rather

irritated than terrified the lads, and they began to pelt the house with snow-balls and stones. He fired from one of the windows, and killed a boy of eleven years of age. A great excitement was produced among the people, by this unnecessary and most wanton conduct. The funeral of the lad was attended by an immense concourse of the inhabitants; and he was considered a *martyr* in the cause of liberty.

The soldiers, when they left their barracks and strolled about the town, frequently carried large clubs, for the purpose, no doubt, of assaulting the people, though with a pretence for their own safety.

On the second of March, two of them rudely insulted and assaulted a workman at a ropewalk, not far from their barracks; being bravely resisted and beaten off, they soon made another attack, in greater numbers, probably ten or twelve. They were again overpowered by the people at the ropewalk: and a third time came, with about fifty of their fellows, to renew the assault. But they were still vanquished, and received some wounds and bruises in the affray which they had thus wantonly provoked. They appeared yet again with large recruits, and threatened vengeance on the defenceless workmen. But the owner or conductor of the ropewalk met them, and prevailed on them to retire, without making the meditated assault. Perhaps the more discreet among them were satisfied of the impropriety of their conduct, or were fearful of the consequences of another attack. On the third, in the afternoon, several of the soldiers, armed with large clubs, went again to the ropewalk; and after much insolent and threatening language, struck some of the workmen.

In consequence of these various quarrels, and of the violent threats of the soldiers, that they would be avenged, when in truth they had been the rude aggressors, the minds of the citizens were greatly alarmed on the fourth and fifth; and so apprehensive were many of an attack from the military, as threatened, that in some instances they required their children and the female part of their families to remain at home during the evening. [The subsequent events are detailed in the Report and Narrative, which follow.]

# REPORT

OF THE

## COMMITTEE OF THE TOWN OF BOSTON.

The town of Boston now legally convened at Faneuil Hall, have directed us, their committee, to acquaint you of their present miserable situation, occasioned by the exorbitancy of the military power, which, in consequence of the intrigues of wicked and designing men to bring us into a state of bondage and ruin, in direct repugnance to those rights which belong to us as men, and as British subjects, have long since been stationed among us.

The soldiers, ever since the fatal day of their arrival, have treated us with an insolence which discovered in them an early prejudice against us, as being that rebellious people which our implacable enemies had maliciously represented us to be. They landed in the town with all the appearance of hostility! They marched through the town with all the ensigns of triumph! and evidently designed to subject the inhabitants to the severe discipline of a garrison! They have been continuing their enormities by abusing the people, rescuing prisoners out of the hands of justice, and even firing upon the inhabitants in the street, when in the peace of God and the King; and when we have applied for redress in the course of the law of the land, our magistrates and courts of justice have appeared to be overawed by them; and such a degree of mean submission has been shewn to them, as has given the greatest disgust, even to the coolest and most judicious persons in the community. Such has been the general state of the town.

On Friday the 2d instant, a quarrel arose between some soldiers of the 29th, and the rope-makers' journeymen and apprentices, which was carried to that length, as to become dangerous to the lives of each party, many of them being much wounded. This contentious disposition continued until the Monday evening following, when a party of seven or eight soldiers were detached from the main guard, under the command of Captain Preston, and by his orders fired upon the inhabitants promiscuously in King street, without the least warning of their intention, and killed three on the spot; another has since died of his wounds, and others are dangerously, some it is feared mortally, wounded. Captain Preston and his party now are in jail. An inquiry is now making into this unhappy affair; and by some of the evidence, there is reason to apprehend that the soldiers have been made use of by others as instruments in executing a settled plot to massacre the inhabitants. There' had been but a little time before a murder committed in the street by two persons of infamous characters, who had been employed by the commissioners and custom-house officers. In the present instance there are witnesses who swear that when the soldiers fired, several muskets were discharged from the house, where the commissioners' board is kept, before which this shocking tragedy was acted; and a boy, servant of one Manwaring, a petty officer in the customs, has upon oath accused his master of firing a gun upon the people out of a window of the same house, a number of persons being at the same time in the room; and confesses that himself, being threatened with death if he refused, discharged a gun twice by the orders of that company. But as it has been impossible for any person to collect a state of facts hitherto, we are directed by the town to give you this short intimation of the matter for the present, and to entreat your friendship to prevent any ill impressions from being made upon the minds of his Majesty's ministers, and others against the town, by the accounts which the commissioners of the customs and our other enemies may send, until the town shall be able to make a full representation of it, which will be addressed to you by the next conveyance.

This horrid transaction has occasioned the greatest anxiety and distress in the minds of the inhabitants, who have ever since been necessitated to keep their own military watch; and his Majesty's council were so convinced of the imminent danger of the troops being any longer in town, that upon application made by the inhabitants, they immediately and unanimously advised the lieutenant-governor to effect their removal; and Lieutenant-Colonel Dalrymple, the present commanding officer, is now removing all the troops to Castle William.

We are, with strict truth, Sir,
Your most faithful and obedient servants,

JOHN HANCOCK,        WM. PHILLIPS,
SAM. ADAMS,          JOS. WARREN,
W. MOLINEUX,         SAM. PEMBERTON,
JOSHUA HENSHAW,
                        *Committee of the Town of Boston.*

To THOMAS POWNALL, ESQ.

*Boston, March* 12, 1770.

Boston, ss. *At a Meeting of the Freeholders and other Inhabitants of the Town of Boston, duly qualified and legally warned, in public Town-Meeting assembled at Faneuil Hall, on Monday the 12th day of March, Anno Domini,* 1770,—

That article in the warrant, for calling this meeting, viz.: "What steps may be further necessary for obtaining a particular account of all proceedings relative to the massacre in King-street on Monday night last, that a full and just representation may be made thereof?" was read,

Whereupon,

*Voted,* That the Honorable James Bowdoin, Esq., Doctor Joseph Warren, and Samuel Pemberton, Esq., be a committee for this important business; and they are desired to report as soon as may be.

*Attest.*          William Cooper, *Town-Clerk.*

*The following Report, containing a narrative of the late Massacre, is submitted to the Town.*

In the name of the Committee,

James Bowdoin.

*At the Town Meeting held on the 19th of March, 1770, by
adjournment,*

THE aforementioned Report was read and considered, whereupon *voted unanimously,* that the same be accepted, and that
it be immediately printed, and the Committee are desired to
transmit copies thereof, as soon as possible, to the following
gentlemen, viz.: the Right Honorable Isaac Barré, Esq., one
of his Majesty's most Honorable Privy Council, Thomas Pownall, Esq., late Governor of the Massachusetts, William Bollan, Esq., Agent for his Majesty's Council, Dennys DeBerdt,
Esq., Agent for the House of Representatives, Benjamin
Franklin, Esq., LL.D., and Barlow Trecothick, Esq., a member of Parliament for the city of London.

  *Attest.*      WILLIAM COOPER, *Town-Clerk.*

A

# SHORT NARRATIVE

OF THE

# HORRID MASSACRE IN BOSTON,

*Perpetrated in the evening of the fifth day of March, 1770, by soldiers of the Twenty-ninth Regiment, which with the Fourteenth Regiment were then quartered there ; with some observations on the state of things prior to that catastrophe.*

---

It may be a proper introduction to this narrative, briefly to represent the state of things for some time previous to the said Massacre ; and this seems necessary in order to the forming a just idea of the causes of it.

At the end of the late war, in which this province bore so distinguished a part, a happy union subsisted between Great Britain and the colonies. This was unfortunately interrupted by the Stamp Act ; but it was in some measure restored by the repeal of it.* It was again interrupted by other acts of parliament for taxing America ; and by the appointment of a Board of Commissioners, in pursuance of an act, which by the face of it was made for the relief and encouragement of commerce, but which in its operation, it was apprehended, would have, and it has in fact had, a contrary effect. By the said act the said Commissioners were "to be resident in some convenient part of his Majesty's dominions in America." This must be understood to be in some part convenient for the whole. But

* The stamp act was passed 22d of March, 1765 ; and repealed 18th of March, 1766.—D.

it does not appear that, in fixing the place of their residence, the convenience of the whole was at all consulted, for Boston, being very far from the centre of the colonies, could not be the place most convenient for the whole. Judging by the act, it may seem this town was intended to be favored, by the Commissioners being appointed to reside here ; and that the consequence of that residence would be the relief and encouragement of commerce ; but the reverse has been the constant and uniform effect of it; so that the commerce of the town, from the embarrassments in which it has been lately involved, is greatly reduced. For the particulars on this head, see the state of the trade not long since drawn up and transmitted to England by a committee of the merchants of Boston.*

The residence of the Commisssioners here has been detrimental, not only to the commerce, but to the political interests of the town and province ; and not only so, but we can trace from it the causes of the late horrid massacre.† Soon after their arrival here in November, 1767, instead of confining themselves to the proper business of their office, they became partizans of Governor Bernard in his political schemes ; and had the weakness and temerity to infringe upon one of the most essential rights of the house of commons of this province —that of giving their votes with freedom, and not being accountable therefor but to their constituents. One of the members of that house, Capt. Timothy Folgier, having voted in some affair contrary to the mind of the said Commissioners, was for so doing dismissed from the office he held under them.

These proceedings of theirs, the difficulty of access to them on office-business, and a supercilious behavior, rendered them disgustful to people in general, who in consequence thereof treated them with neglect. This probably stimulated them to resent it ; and to make their resentment felt, they and their coadjutor, Governor Bernard, made such representations to his

---

* See Bradford's Mass. State Papers, 124–156.—D.

† This act was passed in June, 1767 ; Charles Paxton, William Burch, Henry Hulton, John Temple, and John Robinson, were the Commissioners.—D.

Majesty's ministers as they thought best calculated to bring the displeasure of the nation upon the town and province ; and in order that those representations might have the more weight, they are said to have contrived and executed plans for exciting disturbances and tumults, which otherwise would probably never have existed ; and, when excited, to have transmitted to the ministry the most exaggerated accounts of them.

These particulars of their conduct his Majesty's Council of this province have fully laid open in their proceeding in council, and in their address to General Gage, in July and October, 1768 ; and in their letter to Lord Hillsborough of the 15th of April, 1769.* Unfortunately for us, they have been too successful in their said representations, which, in conjunction with Governor Bernard's, have occasioned his Majesty's faithful subjects of this town and province to be treated as enemies and rebels, by an invasion of the town by sea and land ; to which the approaches were made with all the circumspection usual where a vigorous opposition is expected.† While the town was surrounded by a considerable number of his Majesty's ships of war, two regiments landed and took possession of it ; and to support these, two other regiments arrived some time after from Ireland ; one of which landed at Castle Island,‡ and the other in the town.

Thus were we, in aggravation of our other embarrassments, embarrassed with troops, forced upon us contrary to our inclination—contrary to the spirit of Magna Charta—contrary

---

* See Bradford's Mass. State Papers, 158–166.—D.

† Gordon remarks, that the British commander in this instance expected resistance from the people, and accordingly the vessels of war in the harbor were lying with springs on their cables, and their guns ready for firing instantly upon the town, in case of the least opposition. The troops began to land at about noon of the 1st of October, 1768, under cover of the cannon of their ships, and having effected their landing without molestation, marched on to the common, with muskets charged, bayonets fixed, drums beating, &c., as if taking possession of a conquered town.—*Gordon,* i. 207.—D.

‡ This fortress, then called *Castle William,* was on Castle Island, nearly three miles S. E. from Boston. In 1798, the fortress was ceded to the United States, and in the following year was named by Pres. Adams, *Fort Independence.*—D.

to the very letter of the Bill of Rights, in which it is declared, that the raising or keeping a standing army within the kingdom in time of peace, unless it be with the consent of parliament, is against law, and without the desire of the civil magistrates, to aid whom was the pretence for sending the troops hither; who were quartered in the town in direct violation of an act of parliament for quartering troops in America; and all this in consequence of the representations of the said Commissioners and the said Governor, as appears by their memorials and letters lately published.

As they were the procuring cause of troops being sent hither, they must therefore be the remote and a blameable cause of all the disturbances and bloodshed that have taken place in consequence of that measure.

But we shall leave them to their own reflections, after observing, that as they had some months before the arrival of the troops, under pretence of safety to their persons, retired from town to the Castle, so after the arrival of the troops, and their being quartered in the town, they thought proper to return; having answered, as they doubtless thought, the purpose of their voluntary flight.

We shall next attend to the conduct of the troops, and to some circumstances relative to them. Governor Bernard without consulting the Council, having given up the State House* to the troops at their landing, they took possession of the chambers, where the representatives of the province and the courts of law held their meetings; and (except the council-chamber) of all other parts of that house; in which they continued a considerable time, to the great annoyance of those courts while they sat, and of the merchants and gentlemen of the town, who had always made the lower floor of it their exchange. They had a right so to do, as the property of it was in the town; but they were deprived of that right by mere power. The said Governor soon after, by every stratagem and by every method but a forcibly entry, endeavored to get possession of the manufactory-house,† to make a barrack of it

---

* In State street, now standing.—D.
† The manufactory-house was an old building out of repair, belonging to

for the troops; and for that purpose caused it to be besieged by the troops, and the people in it to be used very cruelly; which extraordinary proceedings created universal uneasiness, arising from the apprehension that the troops under the influence of such a man would be employed to effect the most dangerous purposes; but failing of that, other houses were procured, in which, contrary to act of parliament, he caused the troops to be quartered. ✻ After their quarters were settled, the main guard was posted at one of the said houses, directly opposite to, and not twelve yards from, the State House, (where the General Court, and all the law courts for the county were held), with two field pieces pointed to the State House. This situation of the main guard and field pieces seemed to indicate an attack upon the constitution, and a defiance of law; and to be intended to affront the legislative and executive authority of the province.

The General Court, at the first session after the arrival of the troops, viewed it in this light, and applied to Governor Bernard to cause such a nuisance to be removed; but to no purpose. Disgusted at such an indignity, and at the appearance of being under duresse, they refused to do business in such circumstances; and in consequence thereof were adjourned to Cambridge, to the great inconvenience of the members.

Besides this, the challenging the inhabitants by sentinels posted in all parts of the town before the lodgings of officers, which (for about six months, while it lasted), occasioned many quarrels and uneasiness.✻

Capt. Wilson, of the 59th, exciting the negroes of the town to take away their masters' lives and property, and repair to the army for protection, which was fully proved against him. The attack of a party of soldiers on some of the magistrates

the province. It occupied the site of Hamilton Place. The Council refusing to allow it to be used as a barrack, Governor Bernard directed a British officer to take possession of it. The keeper resisted, with so much resolution, that the attempt was abandoned.—D.

✻ While the British troops were in Boston, the citizens, whenever it was necessary to be out in the evening, generally went armed with walking-sticks, clubs, &c., to protect themselves from insult.—D.

2

of the town—the repeated rescues of soldiers from peace officers—the firing of a loaded musket in a public street, to the endangering a great number of peaceable inhabitants—the frequent wounding of persons by their bayonets and cutlasses, and the numerous instances of bad behavior in the soldiery, made us early sensible that the troops were not sent here for any benefit to the town or province, and that we had no good to expect from such conservators of the peace.*

It was not expected, however, that such an outrage and massacre, as happened here on the evening of the fifth instant, would have been perpetrated. There were then killed and wounded, by a discharge of musketry, eleven of his Majesty's subjects, viz. :

Mr. Samuel Gray, killed on the spot by a ball entering his head.†

Crispus Attucks, a mulatto, killed on the spot, two balls entering his breast.

Mr. James Caldwell, killed on the spot, by two balls entering his back.

Mr. Samuel Maverick, a youth of seventeen years of age, mortally wounded ; he died the next morning.

Mr. Patrick Carr mortally wounded ; he died the 14th instant.

Christopher Monk and John Clark, youths about seventeen years of age, dangerously wounded. It is apprehended they will die.

Mr. Edward Payne, merchant, standing at his door ; wounded.

Messrs. John Green, Robert Patterson, and David Parker ; all dangerously wounded.‡

* The inhabitants instead of making application to the military officers on these occasions, chose rather to oppose the civil authority and the laws of the land to such offenders ; and had not the soldiery found means to evade legal punishments, it is more than probable their insolence would have received a check, and some of the most melancholy effects of it been prevented.

† Samuel Gray was a young man, and worked in the rope-walks of John Gray. "After Mr. Gray had been shot through the body, and had fallen upon the ground, a bayonet was pushed through his skull, and his brains scattered upon the pavement."—*Warren's Address, March 6, 1775.*—D.

‡ The funeral of the victims of the massacre was attended on Thursday,

The actors in this dreadful tragedy were a party of soldiers commanded by Capt. Preston of the 29th regiment. This party, including the Captain, consisted of eight, who are all committed to jail.

There are depositions in this affair which mention, that several guns were fired at the same time from the Custom-house ;* before which this shocking scene was exhibited. Into this matter inquisition is now making. In the meantime it may be proper to insert here the substance of some of those depositions.

Benjamin Frizell, on the evening of the 5th of March, having taken his station near the west corner of the Custom-house in King street, before and at the time of the soldiers firing their guns, declares (among other things) that the first discharge was only of one gun, the next of two guns, upon which he the deponent thinks he saw a man stumble ; the third discharge was of three guns, upon which he thinks he saw two men fall ; and immediately after were discharged five guns, two of which were by soldiers on his right hand ; the other three, as appeared to the deponent, were discharged from the balcony, or the chamber window of the Custom-house, the flashes appearing on the left hand, and higher than the right hand flashes appeared to be, and of which the deponent was very sensible, although his eyes were much turned to the soldiers, who were all on his right hand.

Gillam Bass, being in King street at the same time, declares that they (the party of soldiers from the main guard) posted

the 8th of March. On this occasion the shops of the town were closed, and all the bells were ordered to be tolled, as were those of the neighboring towns. The procession began to move between 4 and 5 o'clock P.M.; the bodies of the two strangers, *Caldwell* and *Attucks*, being borne from Faneuil Hall, and those of the other victims, from the residences of their families—the hearses meeting in King street, near the scene of the tragedy, and passing through the main street, attended by an immense throng, to the burial-ground, where the bodies were all deposited in one vault. *Patrick Carr*, who died of his wounds on the 14th, was buried on the 17th, in the same vault with his murdered associates.—D.

* The Custom-house stood at the corner of King street and Wilson's Lane, the present site of the Merchants' Bank. On the opposite corner stood the Royal Exchange Tavern.—D.

themselves between the Custom-house door and the west corner of it; and in a few minutes began to fire upon the people: two or three of the flashes so high above the rest, that he the deponent verily believes they must have come from the Custom-house windows.

Jeremiah Allen declares, that in the evening of the 5th day of March current, being at about nine o'clock in the front chamber in the house occupied by Col. Ingersoll in King street, he heard some guns' fired, which occasioned his going into the balcony of the said house. That when he was in the said balcony in company with Mr. William Molineux, jun., and John Simpson, he heard the discharge of four or five guns, the flashes of which appeared to be to the westward of the sentry-box, and immediately after, he the deponent heard two or three more guns and saw the flashes thereof from out of the house, now called the Custom-house, as they evidently appeared to him, and which he the said deponent at the same time declared to the aforesaid Molineux and Simpson, being then near him, saying to them, (at the same time pointing his hand towards the Custom-house), "there they are out of the Custom-house."

George Coster, being in King street at the time above-mentioned, declares that in five or six minutes after he stopped, he heard the word of command given to the soldiers, *fire;* upon which one gun was fired, which did no execution, as the deponent observed; about half a minute after two guns, one of which killed one Samuel Gray, a ropemaker, the other a mulatto man, between which two men the deponent stood, after this the deponent heard the discharge of four or five guns more, by the soldiers; immediately after which the deponent heard the discharge of two guns or pistols, from an open window of the middle story of the Custom-house, near to the place where the sentry-box is placed, and being but a small distance from the window, he heard the people from within speak and laugh, and soon after saw the casement lowered down; after which the deponent assisted others in carrying off one of the corpses.

Cato, a negro man, servant to Tuthill Hubbart, Esq., declares that on Monday evening the 5th of March current, on hearing the cry of fire, he ran into King street, where he saw a number of people assembled before the Custom-house; that he stood near the sentry-box and saw the soldiers fire on the people, who stood in the middle of said street; directly after which he saw two flashes of guns, one quick upon the other, from the chamber-window of the Custom-house; and that after the firing was all over, while the people were carrying away the dead and wounded, he saw the Custom-house door opened, and several soldiers (one of whom had a cutlass), go into the Custom-house and shut the door after them.

Benjamin Andrews declares, that being desired by the committee of inquiry to take the ranges of the holes made by musket balls, in two houses nearly opposite to the Custom-house, he finds the bullet hole in the entry-door post of Mr. Payne's house (and which grazed the edge of the door, before it entered the post, where it lodged, two and a half inches deep), ranges just under the stool of the westernmost lower chamber window of the Custom-house.

Samuel Drowne, towards the end of his deposition (which contains a pretty full account of the proceedings of the soldiers on the evening of the 5th instant), declares, that he saw the flashes of two guns fired from the Custom-house, one of which was out of a window of the chamber westward of the balcony, and the other from the balcony; the gun (which he clearly discerned), being pointed through the ballisters, and the person who held the gun, in a stooping posture withdrew himself into the house, having a handkerchief or some kind of cloth over his face.

These depositions show clearly that a number of guns were fired from the Custom-house. As this affair is now inquiring into, all the notice we shall take of it is, that it distinguishes the actors in it into street-actors and house-actors; which is necessary to be observed.

✳ What gave occasion to the melancholy event of that evening seems to have been this. A difference having happened near Mr. Gray's ropewalk,* between a soldier and a man be-

* Gray's ropewalk was near Green's barracks in Atkinson street.—D.

longing to it, the soldier challenged the ropemakers to a box-ing match. The challenge was accepted by one of them, and the soldier worsted. He ran to the barrack in the neighbor-hood, and returned with several of his companions. The fray was renewed, and the soldiers were driven off. They soon returned with recruits and were again worsted. This hap-pened several times, till at length a considerable body of sol-diers was collected, and they also were driven off, the rope-makers having been joined by their brethren of the contiguous ropewalks. By this time Mr. Gray being alarmed interposed, and with the assistance of some gentlemen prevented any fur-ther disturbance. To satisfy the soldiers and punish the man who had been the occasion of the first difference, and as an example to the rest, he turned him out of his service; and waited on Col. Dalrymple, the commanding officer of the troops, and with him concerted measures for preventing fur-ther mischief. Though this affair ended thus, it made a strong impression on the minds of the soldiers in general, who thought the honor of the regiment concerned to revenge those repeated repulses. For this purpose they seem to have formed a com-bination to commit some outrage upon the inhabitants of the town indiscriminately; and this was to be done on the eve-ning of the 5th instant or soon after; as appears by the depo-sitions of the following persons, viz.:

William Newhall declares, that on Thursday night the 1st of March instant, he met four soldiers of the 29th regiment, and that he heard them say, "there were a great many that would eat their dinners on Monday next, that should not eat any on Tuesday."

Daniel Calfe declares, that on Saturday evening the 3d of March, a camp-woman, wife to James McDeed, a grenadier of the 29th, came into his father's shop, and the people talking about the affrays at the ropewalks, and blaming the soldiers for the part they had acted in it, the woman said, "the sol-diers were in me right;" adding, "that before Tuesday or Wednesday night they would wet their swords or bayonets in New England people's blood."

Mary Brailsford declares, that on Sabbath evening the 4th

of March instant, a soldier came to the house of Mr. Amos Thayer, where she then was. He desiring to speak with Mr. Thayer, was told by Mrs. Mary Thayer, that her brother was engaged, and could not be spoke with. He said, "your brother as you call him, is a man I have a great regard for, and I came on purpose to tell him to keep in his house, for before Tuesday night next at twelve o'clock, there will be a great deal of bloodshed, and a great many lives lost;" and added, "that he came out of a particular regard to her brother to advise him to keep in his house, for then he would be out of harm's way." He said, "your brother knows me very well ; my name is Charles Malone." He then went away. Of the same import, and in confirmation of this declaration, are the depositions of Mary Thayer and Asa Copeland, who both live with the said Mr. Thayer, and heard what the soldier said as above-mentioned. It is also confirmed by the deposition of Nicholas Ferriter.

Jane Usher declares, that about 9 o'clock on Monday morning the 5th of March current, from a window she saw two persons in the habit of soldiers, one of whom being on horseback appeared to be an officer's servant. The person on the horse first spoke to the other, but what he said, she is not able to say, though the window was open, and she not more than twenty feet distant; the other replied, "he hoped he should see blood enough spilt before morning."

Matthew Adams declares, that on Monday evening the 5th of March instant, between the hours of 7 and 8 o'clock, he went to the house of Corporal Pershall of the 29th regiment, near Quaker Lane,* where he saw the Corporal and his wife, with one of the fifers of said regiment. When he had got what he went for, and was coming away, the corporal called him back, and desired him with great earnestness to go home to his master's house as soon as business was over, and not to be abroad on any account that night in particular, for "the soldiers were determined to be revenged on the ropewalk people ; and that much mischief would be done." Upon which the fifer (about eighteen or nineteen years of age), said,

* Congress street.

"he hoped in God they would burn the town down." On this he left the house, and the said Corporal called after him again, and begged he would mind what he said to him.

Caleb Swan declares, that on Monday night, the 5th of March instant, at the time of the bells ringing for fire, he heard a woman's voice, whom he knew to be the supposed wife of one Montgomery, a grenadier of the 29th regiment, standing at her door, and heard her say, "it was not fire ; the town was too haughty and too proud; and that many of their arses would be laid low before the morning."

Margaret Swansborough declares, that a free woman named Black Peg, who has kept much with the soldiers, on hearing the disturbance on Monday evening the 5th instant, said, "the soldiers were not to be trod upon by the inhabitants, but would know before morning, whether they or the inhabitants were to be masters."

Joseph Hooton, jun., declares, that coming from the South-end of Boston on Monday evening the 5th of March instant, against Dr. Sewall's meeting he heard a great noise and tumult, with the cry of murder often repeated. Proceeding towards the town-house he was passed by several soldiers running that way, with naked cutlasses and bayonets in their hands. He asked one of them what was the matter, and was answered by him, "by God you shall all know what is the matter soon." Between 9 and 10 o'clock he went into King street, and was present at the tragical scene exhibited near the Custom-house ; as particularly set forth in his deposition.

Mrs. Mary Russell declares, that John Brailsford a private soldier of the fourteenth regiment, who had frequently been employed by her (when he was ordered with his company to the Castle, in consequence of the murders committed by the soldiers on the evening of the 5th of March), coming to the deponent's house declared, that *their* regiment were *ordered* to hold themselves in readiness, and accordingly was ready *that evening*, upon the inhabitants firing on the soldiery, to come to the assistance of the soldiery. On which she asked him, if he would have fired upon any of the inhabitants of this town. To which he replied, " yes, if he had orders ; but that if he saw Mr. Russell, he would have fired wide of him." He also said, "It's well there was no gun fired by the inhabitants, for had there been, *we* should have come to the soldiers' assistance."

⚹ By the foregoing depositions it appears very clearly, there was a general combination among the soldiers of the 29th regiment at least, to commit some extraordinary act of violence upon the town; that if the inhabitants attempted to repel it by firing even one gun upon those soldiers, the 14th regiment were ordered to be in readiness to assist them; and that on the late butchery in King street they actually were ready for that purpose, had a single gun been fired on the perpetrators of it.

It appears by a variety of depositions, that on the same evening between the hours of six and half after nine (at which time the firing began), many persons, without the least provocation, were in various parts of the town insulted and abused by parties of armed soldiers partrolling the streets; particularly:

Mr. Robert Pierpont declares, that between the hours of 7 and 8 in the same evening, three armed soldiers passing him, one of them who had a bayonet gave him a back-handed stroke with it. On complaint of this treatment, he said the deponent should soon hear more of it, and threatened him very hard.

Mr. Henry Bass declares, that at 9 o'clock, a party of soldiers came out of Draper's alley, leading to and from Murray's barracks,* and they being armed with large naked cutlasses, made at every body coming in their way, cutting and slashing, and that he himself very narrowly escaped receiving a cut from the foremost of them, who pursued him.

Samuel Atwood declares, that ten or twelve soldiers armed with drawn cutlasses bolted out of the alley leading from Murray's barracks into Dock-square, and met the deponent,

---

* Murray's barracks were in Brattle street, in the building directly opposite the little alley (formerly called Boylstone's alley), which leads from the bottom of Cornhill. The City Tavern now occupies the site. The 14th royal regiment was here quartered. The 29th was quartered in Water and Atkinson streets.—D.

who asked them if they intended to murder people? They answered, " Yes, by God, root and branch;" saying, "here is one of them;" with that one of them struck the deponent with a club, which was repeated by another. The deponent being unarmed turned to go off, and he received a wound on the left shoulder, which reached the bone, disabled him, and gave him much pain. Having gone a few steps the deponent met two officers, and asked them, "Gentlemen, what is the matter?" they answered, " You will see by and by;" and as he passed by Col. Jackson's he heard the cry, turn out the guards.

Capt. James Kirkwood declares, that about 9 of the clock in the evening of the 5th day of March current, he was going by Murray's barracks : hearing a noise he stopped at Mr. Rhoads's door, opposite the said barracks, where said Rhoads was standing, and stood some time, and saw the soldiers coming out of the yard from the barracks, armed with cutlasses and bayonets, and rushing through Boylstone's alley* into Cornhill, two officers, namely, Lieuts. Minchin and Dickson, came out of the mess-house, and said to the soldiers, " My lads, come into the barracks and don't hurt the inhabitants," and then retired into the mess-house. Soon after they came to the door again, and found the soldiers in the yard ; and directly upon it, Ensign Mall came to the gate of the barrack-yard and said to the soldiers, " Turn out, and I will stand by you ;" this he repeated frequently, adding, " Kill them! stick them! knock them down; run your bayonets through them ;" with a great deal of language of like import. Upon which a great number of soldiers came out of the barracks with naked cutlasses, headed by said Mall, and went through the aforesaid alley ; that some officers came and got the soldiers into their barracks, and that Mall, with his sword or cutlass drawn in his hand, as often had them out again, but were at last drove into their barracks by the aforesaid Minchin and Dickson.

Mr. Henry Rhoads's declaration agrees with Captain Kirkwood's.

Mr. Matthias King, of Halifax, in Nova Scotia, declares, that

* The arch-way through the block from Brattle street to Cornhill.—D.

in the evening of the fifth day of March instant, about nine o'clock, he was at his lodgings at Mrs. Torrey's, near the town pump, and heard the bells ring and the cry of "Fire;" upon which he went to the door and saw several soldiers come round the south side of the town-house, armed with bayonets, and something which he took to be broadswords; that one of those people came up almost to him and Mr. Bartholomew Kneeland; and that they had but just time to shut the door upon him; otherwise he is well assured they must have fell victims to their boundless cruelty. He afterwards went into the upper chamber of the said house, and was looking out of the window when the drum and the guard went to the barrack, and he saw one of the guards kneel and present his piece, with a bayonet fixed, and heard him swear he would fire upon a parcel of boys who were then in the street, but he did not. He further declares that when the body of troops was drawn up before the guard house (which was presently after the massacre), he heard an officer say to another, that this was fine work, and just what he wanted; but in the hurry he could not see him, so as to know him again.

Robert Polley declares, that on Monday evening, the 5th instant, as he was going home, he observed about ten persons standing near Mr. Taylor's door; after standing there a small space of time, he went with them towards Boylston's alley, opposite to Murray's barracks; we met in the alley about eight or nine armed soldiers; they assaulted us, and gave us a great deal of abusive language; we then drove them back to the barracks with sticks only; we looked for stones or bricks, but could find none, the ground being covered with snow. Some of the lads dispersed, and he, the said Polley, with a few others, were returning peaceably home, when we met about nine or ten other soldiers armed : one of them said, "Where are the sons of bitches?" They struck at several persons in the street, and went towards the head of the alley. Two officers came and endeavored to get them into their barracks; one of the lads proposed to ring the bell; the soldiers went through the alley, and the boys huzzaed, and said they were gone through Royal Exchange lane into King street.

Samuel Drowne declares that, about nine o'clock of the evening of the fifth of March current, standing at his own door in Cornhill, he saw about fourteen or fifteen soldiers of the 29th regiment, who came from Murray's barracks, armed with naked cutlasses, swords, &c., and came upon the inhabitants of the town, then standing or walking in Cornhill, and abused some, and violently assaulted others as they met them; most of whom were without so much as a stick in their hand to defend themselves, as he very clearly could discern, it being moonlight, and himself being one of the assaulted persons. All or most of the said soldiers he saw go into King street (some of them through Royal Exchange lane),* and there followed them, and soon discovered them to be quarrelling and fighting with the people whom they saw there, which he thinks were not more than a dozen, when the soldiers came first, armed as aforesaid. Of those dozen people, the most of them were gentlemen, standing together a little below the Town House, upon the Exchange. At the appearance of those soldiers so armed, the most of the twelve persons went off, some of them being first assaulted.

The violent proceedings of this party, and their going into King street, "quarrelling and fighting with the people whom they saw there" (mentioned in Mr. Drowne's deposition), was immediately introductory to the grand catastrophe.

These assailants, who issued from Murray's barracks (so called), after attacking and wounding divers persons in Cornhill, as above-mentioned, being armed, proceeded (most of them) up the Royal Exchange lane into King street; where, making a short stop, and after assaulting and driving away the few they met there, they brandished their arms and cried out, "Where are the boogers! where are the cowards!" At this time there were very few persons in the street beside themselves. This party in proceeding from Exchange lane into King street, must pass the sentry posted at the westerly corner of the Custom House, which butts on that lane and fronts on that street. This is needful to be mentioned, as near that spot and

* Exchange street.

in that street the bloody tragedy was acted, and the street actors in it were stationed : their station being but a few feet from the front side of the said Custom House. The outrageous behavior and the threats of the said party occasioned the ringing of the meeting-house bell near the head of King street, which bell ringing quick, as for fire, it presently brought out a number of the inhabitants, who being soon sensible of the occasion of it, were naturally led to King street, where the said party had made a stop but a little while before, and where their stopping had drawn together a number of boys, round the sentry at the Custom House. Whether the boys mistook the sentry for one of the said party, and thence took occasion to differ with him, or whether he first affronted them, which is affirmed in several depositions,—however that may be, there was much foul language between them, and some of them, in consequence of his pushing at them with his bayonet, threw snowballs at him,* which occasioned him to knock hastily at the door of the Custom House. From hence two persons thereupon proceeded immediately to the main-guard, which was posted opposite to the State House, at a small distance, near the head of the said street. The officer on guard was Capt. Preston, who with seven or eight soldiers, with fire-arms and charged bayonets, issued from the guard-house, and in great haste posted himself and his soldiers in front of the Custom House, near the corner aforesaid. In passing to this station the soldiers pushed several persons with

* Since writing this narrative, several depositions have appeared, which make it clear that the sentry was first in fault. He overheard a barber's boy saying, that a captain of the 14th (who had just passed by) was so mean a fellow as not to pay his barber for shaving him. Upon this the sentry left his post and followed the boy into the middle of the street, where he told him to show his face. The boy pertly replied, " I am not ashamed to show my face to any man." Upon this the sentry gave him a sweeping stroke on the head with his musket, which made him reel and stagger, and cry much. A fellow-apprentice asked the sentry what he meant by this abuse ? He replied, " Damn your blood, if you do not get out of the way I will give you something ;" and then fixed his bayonet and pushed at the lads, who both ran out of his way. This dispute collected a few persons about the boy, near the Custom House. Presently after this, the party above-mentioned came into King street, which was a further occasion of drawing people thither, as above related.—See deposition of Benjamin Broaders and others.

their bayonets, driving through the people in so rough a manner that it appeared they intended to create a disturbance. This occasioned some snowballs to be thrown at them, which seems to have been the only provocation that was given. Mr. Knox (between whom and Capt. Preston there was some conversation on the spot) declares, that while he was talking with Capt. Preston, the soldiers of his detachment had attacked the people with their bayonets; and that there was not the least provocation given to Capt. Preston or his party; the backs of the people being toward them when the people were attacked. He also declares, that Capt. Preston seemed to be in great haste and much agitated, and that, according to his opinion, there were not then present in King street above seventy or eighty persons at the extent.

The said party was formed into a half circle; and within a short time after they had been posted at the Custom House, began to fire upon the people.

Captain Preston is said to have ordered them to fire, and to have repeated that order. One gun was fired first; then others in succession, and with deliberation, till ten or a dozen guns were fired; or till that number of discharges were made from the guns that were fired. By which means eleven persons were killed and wounded, as above represented.

These facts, with divers circumstances attending them, are supported by the depositions of a considerable number of persons, and among others of the following, viz. :—Messrs. Henry Bass, Samuel Atwood, Samuel Drowne, James Kirkwood, Robert Polley, Samuel Condon, Daniel Usher, Josiah Simpson, Henry Knox, Gillam Bass, John Hickling, Richard Palmes, Benjamin Frizzel, and others, whose depositions are in the Appendix.

Soon after the firing, a party from the main guard went with a drum to Murray's and the other barracks, beating an alarm as they went, which, with the firing, had the effect of a signal for action. Whereupon all the soldiers of the 29th regiment, or the main body of them, appeared in King street under arms, and seemed bent on a further massacre of the inhabitants, which was with great difficulty prevented. They were drawn up between the State House and main guard, their lines extending across the street and facing down King street, where the town-people were assembled.  The first line kneeled, and the whole of the first platoon presented their guns ready to fire, as soon as the word should be given.  They continued in that posture a considerable time; but by the good providence of God they were restrained from firing.  That they then went into King street with such a disposition will appear probable by the two following depositions.

Mrs. Mary Gardner, living in Atkinson street, declares, that on Monday evening the 5th of March current, and before the guns fired in King street, there were a number of soldiers assembled from Green's barracks towards the street, and opposite to her gate; that they stood very still until the guns were fired in King street; then they clapped their hands and gave a cheer, saying, "This is all that we want."  They ran to their barrack, and came out again in a few minutes, all with their arms, and ran towards King street.

William Fallass declares, that (after the murder in King street) on the evening of the 5th instant, upon his return home, he had occasion to stop opposite to the lane leading to Green's barracks,* and while he stood there, the soldiers rushed by him with their arms, towards King street, saying, "This is our time or chance:" and that he never saw men or dogs so greedy for their prey as those soldiers seemed to be, and the sergeants could hardly keep them in their ranks.

These circumstances, with those already mentioned, amount to a clear proof of a combination among them to commit some outrage upon the town on that evening; and that after the enormous one committed in King street, they intended to add to the horrors of that night by making a further slaughter.

At the time Capt. Preston's party issued from the main guard, there were in King street about two hundred persons, and those were collected there by the ringing of the bell in consequence of the violences of another party, that had been there a very little while before.  When Captain Preston had got to the Custom-house, so great a part of the people dispersed

---

* In Atkinson street.—D.

at sight of the soldiers, that not more than twenty or thirty
then remained in King street, as Mr. Drowne declares,* and
at the time of the firing not seventy, as Mr. Palmes thinks.†

But after the firing, and when the slaughter was known,
which occasioned the ringing of all the bells of the town, a
large body of the inhabitants soon assembled in King street,
and continued there the whole time the 29th regiment was
there under arms, and would not retire till that regiment, and
all the soldiers that appeared, were ordered, and actually went,
to their barracks: after which, having been assured by the
Lieutenant-Governor, and a number of the civil magistrates
present, that every legal step should be taken to bring the
criminals to justice, they gradually dispersed. For some time
the appearance of things were dismal. The soldiers outrageous on the one hand, and the inhabitants justly incensed
against them on the other: both parties seemed disposed to
come to action. In this case the consequences would have
been terrible. But by the interposition of his Honor, some of
his Majesty's council, a number of civil magistrates, and other
gentlemen of weight and influence, who all endeavored to
calm and pacify the people, and by the two principal officers
interposing their authority with regard to the soldiers, there
was happily no further bloodshed ensued ; and by two o'clock
the town was restored to a tolerable state of quiet. About
that time, Capt. Preston, and a few hours after, the party that
had fired, were committed to safe custody.

 One happy effect has arisen from this melancholy affair,
and it is the general voice of the town and province it may
be a lasting one—all the troops are removed from the town.
They are quartered for the present in the barracks at Castle-
Island; from whence it is hoped they will have a speedy order
to remove entirely out of the province, together with those
persons who were the occasion of their coming hither.

In what manner this was effected, it is not foreign from the
subject of this narrative to relate.

The morning after the massacre, a town-meeting was held ;
at which attended a very great number of the freeholders and

other inhabitants of the town.   They were deeply impressed and affected by the tragedy of the preceding night, and were unanimously of opinion, it was incompatible with their safety that the troops should remain any longer in the town.   In consequence thereof they chose a committee of fifteen gentlemen to wait upon his Honor the Lieutenaht-Governor in Council, to request of him to issue his orders for the immediate removal of the troops.

The message was in these words:
" That it is the unanimous opinion of this meeting that the inhabitants and soldiery can no longer live together in safety ; that nothing can rationally be expected to restore the peace of the town and prevent further blood and carnage, but the immediate removal of the troops ; and that we therefore most fervently pray his Honor, that his power and influence may be exerted for their instant removal."

His Honor's reply, which was laid before the town then adjourned to the old south meeting-house, was as follows :

" Gentlemen,
" I am extremely sorry for the unhappy differences between the inhabitants and troops, and especially for the action of the last evening, and I have exerted myself upon that occasion, that a due inquiry may be made, and that the law may have its course.   I have in council consulted with the commanding officers of the two regiments who are now in the town.   They have their orders from the General at New York.   It is not in my power to countermand those orders.   The Council have desired that the two regiments may be removed to the Castle. From the particular concern which the 29th regiment has had in your differences, Col. Dalrymple, who is the commanding officer of the troops, has signified that that regiment shall without delay be placed in the barracks at the castle, until he can send to the General and receive his further orders concerning both the regiments, and that the main-guard shall be removed, and the 14th regiment so disposed, and laid under such re-

3

straint, that all occasion of future disturbances may be prevented."

The foregoing reply having been read and fully considered —the question was put, Whether the report be satisfactory? Passed in the negative (only one dissentient) out of upwards of 4,000 voters.

A respectable committee was then appointed to wait on his Honor the Lieutenant-Governor, and inform him, that it is the unanimous opinion of this meeting, that the reply made to a vote of the inhabitants presented his Honor in the morning, is by no means satisfactory; and that nothing less will satisfy than a total and immediate removal of all the troops.

The committee having waited upon the Lieutenant-Governor, agreeable to the foregoing vote, laid before the inhabitants the following vote of Council received from his Honor.

His Honor the Lieutenant-Governor laid before the Board a vote of the town'of Boston, passed this afternoon, and then addressed the Board as follows:

"Gentlemen of the Council,

"I lay before you a vote of the town of Boston, which I have just now received from them, and I now ask your advice what you judge necessary to be done upon it."

The Council thereupon expressed themselves to be unanimously of opinion, "that it was absolutely necessary for his Majesty's service, the good order of the town, and the peace of the province, that the troops should be immediately removed out of the town of Boston, and thereupon advised his Honor to communicate this advice of the Council to Col. Dalrymple, and to pray that he would order the troops down to Castle William." The committee also informed the town, that Col. Dalrymple, after having seen the vote of Council, said to the committee,

"That he now gave his word of honor that he would begin his preparations in the morning, and that there should be no unnecessary delay until the whole of the two regiments were removed to the Castle."

Upon the above report being read, the inhabitants could not avoid expressing the high satisfaction it afforded them.*

After measures were taken for the security of the town in the night by a strong military watch, the meeting was dissolved.

------------•◦•◦•------------

In the concluding paragraph of the foregoing narrative it is said, that the town-meeting was dissolved after the measures were taken for the security of the town in the night, by a strong military watch.

Our implacable enemies, in pursuance of their plan of misrepresentation, have taken pains to misrepresent this most necessary measure, by declaring it to have been contrary to the mind of the Commander-in-Chief, and against law.

This matter will be judged of, by stating the fact, and producing the law.

When the Committee, who had waited on the Lieutenant-Governor, had reported to the town that the troops would be removed to Castle Island (at which time it was near night), it was thought necessary for the safety of the town, and for preventing a rescue of the persons committed to jail for firing upon and killing a number of his Majesty's subjects, that there should be a military watch; and divers gentlemen were desired to take the needful steps for that purpose. It being then night, it was impossible a regular notification should issue from the officers of the militia; a considerable number of respectable persons therefore offered themselves volunteers, and did the duty of a military watch under the direction of the Lieut.-Colonel, who attended that service with the approbation of the chief Colonel of the Bos-

* * The town of Boston afterwards determined to celebrate the anniversary of the fifth of March, to the end that there might be an annual development of the "fatal effects of the policy of standing armies, and the natural tendency of quartering regular troops in populous cities in times of peace." The first anniversary was observed at the Manufactory House, that being the place where the first opposition to the soldiery was made, in October, 1768. The anniversary was observed every year until 1784, when the celebration was superseded by that of the 4th July. The names of the orators in their order were—James Lovell, Dr. Joseph Warren, Dr. Benjamin Church, John Hancock, Dr. Joseph Warren, Rev. Peter Thacher, Benjamin Hichborn, Jonathan W. Austin, William Tudor, Jonathan Mason, Jun., Thomas Dawes, Jun., George Richards Minot, Dr. Thomas Welch. The "Boston Orations," so called, were published in a volume in 1785, by Peter Edes.—D.

ton regiment. The next day, with two of the select men of the town, the chief Colonel went to the Lieutenant-Governor, and they informed him it was apprehended absolutely necessary for the safety of the town there should be a military watch kept ; and that the Colonel then waited upon him to receive his orders. The Lieutenant-Governor declined giving any orders concerning it, but said the law was clear, that the Colonel, as chief officer of the regiment, might order a military watch ; and that he might do about it as he thought fit. In consequence of this, and knowing the law gave him such a power, the Colonel issued his orders for that purpose, and a regular watch was kept the following night. The next day the Lieutenant-Governor sent for the Colonel, and let him know, that he was in doubt about the legality of the appointment of the military watch ; and recommended to the Colonel to take good advice, whether he had a right by law to order such a watch.

This being quite unexpected, occasioned the Colonel to express himself with some fervor. He also said, he had already taken advice, and had no doubt of his own power ; but had the preceding day waited upon his Honor as Commander-in-Chief to receive his orders ; which, as his Honor had declined giving, and left the matter with himself, he had appointed a military watch ; and judged it a necessary measure to quiet the fears and apprehensions of the town. The interview ended with the Lieut.-Governor's recommending again, that the Colonel would take care to proceed according to law ; and without his forbidding a military watch.

This military watch was continued every night, till Colonel Dalrymple had caused the two regiments under his command to be removed to the barracks at Castle Island. During the continuance of the watch, the Justices of the Peace in their turns attended every night ; and the utmost order and regularity took place through the whole of it.

This is the state of the fact, upon which every one is left to make his own observations.

Now for the law ; with respect to which nothing is more necessary than just to recite it. It runs thus, "That there be military watches appointed and kept in every town, at such times, in such places, and in such numbers, and under such regulation, as the chief military officers of each town shall appoint, or as they may receive orders from the chief officer of the regiment."* This needs no comment. It clearly authorizes the chief officer of the regiment to appoint military watches. The late military watch in Boston being founded on such an appointment was therefore according to law.

* See a Law of the Province for regulating the Militia, made in the 5th year of William and Mary, Chap. 7., Sec. 10.

# APPENDIX;

CONTAINING

THE SEVERAL DEPOSITIONS REFERRED TO IN THE PRECEDING NARRATIVE; AND ALSO OTHER DEPOSITIONS RELATIVE TO THE SUBJECT OF IT.

## (No. 1.)

I, John Wilme, of lawful age, testify that about ten days before the late massacre, Christopher Rumbly of the 14th regiment, was at my house at the north part of the town, with sundry other soldiers; and he, the said Rumbly, did talk very much against the town, and said if there should be any interruption, that the grenadiers' company was to march up King-street; and that if any of the inhabitants would join with them, the women should be sent to the castle, or some other place; and that he had been in many a battle; and that he did not know but he might be soon in one here; and that if he was, he would level his piece so as not to miss; and said that the blood would soon run in the streets of Boston; and that one Sumner of the same regiment did say that he came here to make his fortune; and that he would as soon fight for one King as another; and that the two gaps would be stopped, said one of the soldiers; and that they would soon sweep the streets of Boston.

And further saith, that he heard a soldier's wife, named Eleanor Park, say, that if there should be any disturbance in the town of Boston, and that if any of the people were wounded, she would take a stone in her handkerchief and beat their brains out, and plunder the rebels.—And further I say not.                      JOHN WILME.

Suffolk, ss. Boston, March 21, 1770.  John Wilme, above named, after due examination, made oath to the truth of the aforesaid affidavit, taken to perpetuate the remembrance of the thing.

Before, JOHN RUDDOCK, Just. Peace and of the Quorum,
And, JOHN HILL, Just. Peace.

## (No. 2.)

I, Sarah Wilme, of lawful age, testify that about ten days before the late massacre, Christopher Rumbly, of the 14th regiment, was at our house at the north part of the town, with sundry other soldiers: and he, the said Rumbly, did talk very much against the town, and said, if there should be any interruption, that the grenadiers' company was to march up King-street; and that if any of the inhabitants would join with them, the women should be sent to the castle or some other place; and that he had been in many a battle; and that he did not know but he might be soon in one here; and that if he was, he would level his piece so as not to miss; and said that the blood would soon run in the streets of Boston; and that one Sumner, of the same regiment, did say, that he came here to make his fortune, and that he would as soon fight for one King as another; and that the two gaps would be stopped, said one of the soldiers; and that they would soon sweep the streets of Boston.—And further saith not.

SARAH WILME.

Suffolk, ss.    Boston, March 21, 1770.    Sarah Wilme, above named, after due examination, made oath to the truth of the aforesaid affidavit, taken to perpetuate the remembrance of the thing.

Before, JOHN RUDDOCK, Just. Peace and of the Quorum,
And, JOHN TUDOR, Justice Peace.

(No. 3.)

I, David Cockran, of lawful age, testify, that I went to the house of Mr. John Wilme, to pay him a visit in the evening, about ten days before the late massacre, and there I found four or five soldiers, and after some time the said Wilme told me not to be out in the night of such a day (though I cannot positively say what day); whereupon I asked him what he meant, and he told me that there would be disturbances, or words to that effect; and that one of said soldiers took me by the arm, and said, the blood would soon run in the streets of Boston.—And further saith not.

His<br>Attest. ELISHA STORY,              David ⋈ Cockran.<br>Mark.

Suffolk, ss.    Boston, March 21, 1770.    David Cockran, above named, after due examination, made oath to the truth of the aforesaid affidavit, taken to perpetuate the remembrance of the thing.

Before, JOHN RUDDOCK, Just. Peace and of the Quorum,
And, JOHN HILL, Justice Peace.

(No. 4.)

William Newhall, living in Fish-street, of lawful age, testifies and says, that on Thursday night, being the first of March instant, between the market and Justice Quincy's, he met four soldiers of the 29th regiment, all unarmed, and that he heard them say, "there was a great many that would eat their dinners on Monday next, that should not eat any on Tuesday."

WILLIAM NEWHALL.

Suffolk, ss. Boston, March 21, 1770. William Newhall, above-named, after due examination, made oath to the truth of the aforesaid affidavit, taken to perpetuate the remembrance of the thing.

Before, JOHN RUDDOCK, Just. Peace and of the Quorum, And, JOHN HILL, Just. Peace.

---

(No. 5.)

I, Nicholas Feriter, of lawful age, testify that on Friday the second instant, about half past 11 o'clock, A.M., a soldier of the 29th Regiment came to Mr. John Gray's ropewalks, and looking into one of the windows said, *by God I'll have satisfaction!* with many other oaths; at the last he said he was not afraid of any one in the ropewalks. I stept out of the window and speedily knock'd up his heels. On falling, his coat flew open, and a naked sword appeared, which one John Willson, following me out, took from him, and brought into the ropewalks. The soldier then went to Green's barrack, and in about twenty minutes returned with eight or nine more soldiers armed with clubs, and began, as I was told, with three or four men in Mr. Gray's warehouse, asking them why they had abused the soldier aforesaid? These men in the warehouse passed the word down the walk for the hands to come up, which they did, and soon beat them off. In a few minutes the soldiers appeared again at the same place, reinforced to the number of thirty or forty, armed with clubs and cutlasses, and headed by a tall negro drummer with a cutlass chained to his body, with which, at first rencounter, I received a cut on the head, but being immediately supported by nine or ten more of the rope-makers, armed with their wouldring sticks, we again beat them off. And further I say not.

NICHOLAS FERITER.

Suffolk, ss. Boston, March 20, 1770. Nicholas Feriter, above mentioned, after due examination, made oath to the aforesaid affidavit, taken to perpetuate the remembrance of the thing.

Before, JOHN RUDDOCK, Jus. Peace and of the Quorum, And, JOHN HILL, Jus. Peace.

---

(No. 6.)

I, Jeffrey Richardson, of lawful age, testify and say, that on Friday, the second instant, about 11 o'clock, A.M., eight or ten soldiers of the 29th regiment, armed with clubs, came to Mr. John Gray's ropewalks, and challenged all the rope-makers to come out and fight them. All the hands then present, to the number of thirteen or fourteen, turned out with their wouldring sticks, and beat them off directly. They very speedily returned to the ropewalk, reinforced to the number of thirty or forty, and headed by a tall negro drummer, again challenged them out, which the same hands

accepting, again beat them off with considerable bruises. And further I say not.                                    JEFFREY RICHARDSON.
  Suffolk, ss.  Boston, March 19, 1770.  Jeffrey Richardson, above-named, after due examination, made oath to the truth of the above affidavit, taken to perpetuate the remembrance of the thing.
  Before, RI. DANA, Just. of Peace and of the Quorum,
  And, JOHN HILL, Jus. Peace.

-------

(No. 7.)

John Fisher, of lawful age, testifies and saith, that on the second day of March, between 11 and 12 o'clock, A.M., he saw about six soldiers going towards Mr. John Gray's ropewalk, some with clubs ; they had not been there long, before they returned quicker than they went, and retreated into their barracks, and brought out the light infantry company, with many others, and went against the rope-makers again ; but were soon beat off as far as Green's lane, the soldiers following and chasing many persons they could see in the lane with their clubs, and endeavoring to strike them, when a corporal came and ordered them into the barracks. And further saith, that on Saturday the 3rd instant, he saw the soldiers making clubs ; and by what he could understand from their conversation, they were determined to have satisfaction by Monday. And further saith not.                                         JOHN FISHER.
  Suffolk, ss.  Boston, March 17, 1770.  John Fisher, above-named, after due examination, made oath to the truth of the above affidavit, taken to perpetuate the remembrance of the thing.
  Before, RI. DANA, Just. of Peace and of the Quorum,
  And, SAM. PEMBERTON, Just. Peace.

-------

(No. 8.)

I, John Hill, aged sixty-nine, testify, that in the forenoon of Friday the second of March current, I was at a house the corner of a passage way leading from Atkinson's street to Mr. John Gray's rope-walks, near Green's barracks so called, when I saw eight or ten soldiers pass the window with clubs. I immediately got up and went to the door, and found them returning from the rope-walks to the barracks ; whence they again very speedily re-appeared, now increased to the number of thirty or forty, armed with clubs and other weapons. In this latter company was a tall negro drummer, to whom I called, you black rascal, what have you to do with white people's quarrels ? He answered, I suppose I may look on, and went forward. I went out directly and commanded the peace, telling them I was in commission ; but they not regarding me, knocked down a rope-maker in my presence, and two or three of them beating him with clubs, I endeavored to relieve him ; but on approaching the fellows who were mauling him, one of them with a great club struck at me with such violence, that had I not happily avoided it might have been fatal to me. The party last mentioned rushed in towards the rope-walks, and attacked the rope-makers nigh the tar-kettle, but were soon beat off, drove out of the passage-way by which they entered, and were followed by the rope-makers, whom I persuaded to go back, and they readily obeyed. And further I say not. JOHN HILL.

Suffolk, ss. Boston, March 19, 1770. John Hill, Esq., above-named, after due examination, made oath to the truth of the aforesaid affidavit, taken to perpetuate the remembrance of the thing.

Before, RI. DANA, } Justices of the Peace and of the
JOHN RUDDOCK, } Quorum.

---

## (No. 9.)

I, John Gray, of lawful age, testify and say, that on the Saturday preceding the massacre on the Monday evening of the 5th instant, Middleton the chimney-sweeper being at my house, said to my maid, as she informed me, that he was well acquainted with the soldiers, and they had determined to have their revenge of the rope-walk people ; being alarmed with this news, I determined to see Col. Dalrymple on Monday morning. At Sabbath noon I was surprised at hearing that Col. Carr and his officers had entered my rope-walk, opened the windows, doors, &c., giving out that they were searching for a dead sergeant of their regiment ; this put me upon immediately waiting upon Col. Dalrymple, to whom I related what I understood had passed at the rope-walk days before. He replied it was much the same as he had heard from his people ; but says he, " your man was the aggressor in affronting one of my people, by asking him if he wanted to work, and then telling him to clean his little-house." For this expression I dismissed my journeyman on the Monday morning following ; and further said, I would do all in my power to prevent my people's giving them any affront in future. He then assured me, he had and should do everything in his power to keep his soldiers in order, and prevent their any more entering my inclosure. Presently after, Col. Carr came in, and asked Col. Dalrymple what they should do, for they were daily losing their men ; that three of his grenadiers passing quietly by the rope-walks were greatly abused, and one of them so much beat that he would die. He then said he had been searching for a sergeant who had been murdered ; upon which, I said, Yes, Colonel, I hear you have been searching for him in my rope-walks ; and asked him, whether that sergeant had been in the affray there on the Friday ; he replied, no : for he was seen on the Saturday. I then asked him, how he could think of looking for him in my walks ; and that had he applied to me, I would have waited on him, and opened every apartment I had for his satisfaction. JOHN GRAY.

Suffolk, ss. Boston, March 22, 1770. John Gray, above-named, after due examination, made oath to the truth of the above-written affidavit. Taken to perpetuate the remembrance of the thing.

Before, Ri. Dana, Justice of the Peace and of the Quorum,
And, John Hill, Jus. Peace.

---

(No. 10.)

Archibald McNeil, Jun., of lawful age, testifies and says, that on Saturday the third instant, about half an hour after four in the afternoon, the deponent with two apprentices were spinning at the lower end of Mr. McNeil's rope-walk, three stout grenadiers, armed with bludgeons, came to them, and addressing the deponent, said, " You damned dogs, don't you deserved to be killed ? Are you fit to die ?" The deponent and company being quite unarmed, gave no answer. James Bayley, a seafaring young man, coming up, said to the deponent, &c., Why did you not answer ? One of the grenadiers, named Dixson, hearing him, came up to Bayley and asked him if he was minded to vindicate the cause ? Bayley, also unarmed, did not answer till James Young came up, who, though equally naked, said to the grenadier, Damn it, I know what a soldier is. That grenadier stood still, and the other who had threatened the deponent came up and struck at him, which Young fended off with his arms, and then turning, aimed a blow at the deponent, which had it reached might probably have been fatal. Patrick ———, Mr. Winter Calef's journeyman, seeing the affray, went into the tan-house, and bringing out two bats gave one to a bystander, who, together with Patrick, soon cleared the walk of them. And further saith not.                                    ARCHIBALD McNEIL.

Suffolk, ss. Boston, March 17, 1770. Archibald McNeil above named, after due examination, made oath to the above affidavit, taken to perpetuate the remembrance of the thing.

Before, Ri. Dana, Just. of Peace and of the Quorum,
John Hill, Just. of Peace.

---

(No. 11.)

Mary Thayer, of lawful age, testifies and says, that on Sabbath day evening, the 4th current, a soldier of the 29th, named Charles Malone, came into Mr. Amos Thayer's house, brother to the deponent, and sent a young lad belonging to Mr. Thayer up stairs to his master, desiring him to come down to him. Mr. Thayer refused to come down or have any thing to say to him. The deponent going down on other occasion, said she would hear what the soldier had to say. And coming to the soldier told him her brother was engaged. The soldier said, " Your brother as you call him, is a man I have a very great regard for, and came here to desire him to keep in the house and not be out, for there would be a great deal of disturbance and blood between that time and Tuesday night at 12 o'clock." He repeatedly said he had a greater regard for Mr. Thayer than any one in Boston, and on that account came to desire him to keep in the house, which if he did there would be no danger. After repeating the above frequently, he even turned at the door, and said, my name is Charles Malone, your brother knows me well, and insisted very earnestly that the deponent would not neglect informing her brother. And further saith not.

MARY THAYER.

Suffolk, ss. Boston, March 17, 1770. Mary Thayer, above named, after due examination, made oath to the truth of the above affidavit, taken to perpetuate the remembrance of the thing.

Before RI. DANA, Just. of Peace and of the Quorum,
JOHN HILL, Just. of Peace.

---

(No. 12.)

I, Mary Brailsford, of lawful age, testify and declare, that on Sunday evening, the 4th instant, a person knocked at the door of Mr. Thayer's house ; Mr. Thayer's lad went to see who it was, the boy went up stairs to his master, and the soldier came into the room where I then was ; Miss Mary Thayer and the boy came down stairs into the same room. Miss Thayer told the soldier her brother was engaged, and could not be spoke with. He said, "Your brother as you call him, is a man I have great regard for, and I came on purpose to tell him to keep in his house, for before Tuesday night next at twelve o'clock, there will be a great deal of blood shed, and a great many lives lost ;" and added, "that he came out of particular regard to her brother to advise him to keep in his house, for then he would be out of harm's way." He said, your brother knows me very well, my name is Charles Malone ; he then went away.— And further saith not.

her<br>MARY M BRAILSFORD,

Attest. Wm. Palfrey. Mark.

Suffolk, ss. Boston, March 17, 1770. Mary Brailsford above named, after due examination, made oath to the truth of the above written affidavit, taken to perpetuate the remembrance of the thing.

Before RI. DANA, Just. of Peace and of the Quorum,
JOHN HILL, Just. of Peace.

---

(No. 13.)

I, Asa Copeland, of lawful age, testify and declare, that on Sunday evening, the 4th instant, a soldier named Malone, came to the house of my master, Mr. Amos Thayer, and asked for the young man that lived in the house. I asked him what young man he meant ; he said the young man a carpenter ; I supposing he meant my master, told him he was up stairs. He then asked me to go and call him, and said he wanted to speak with him ; I then went up and told my master that Malone was below and wanted to speak with him. My master told me to tell him he was engaged and could not go down, and said if he had any thing to say, he must say it to his sister, Miss Mary Thayer. I then went down and heard said Malone saying to Miss Thayer, " I would have him keep in for I have a greater regard for Mr. Thayer, than for any other person in town ;" and added, " I would have him keep in his own place, for by Tuesday night next before twelve o'clock, there will be a great many lives lost, and a great deal of blood shed, which he repeated several times. As he was going out of the door he turned back and said Mr. Thayer knew him very well, and had drank with him, that his name was Charles Malone. And further saith not.

ASA COPELAND.

Suffolk, ss. Boston, March 17, 1770. Asa Copeland, above named, after due examination, made oath to the truth of the above affidavit, taken to perpetuate the remembrance of the thing.
Before Ri. DANA, Just. of Peace and of the Quorum,
JOHN HILL, Just. of Peace.

---

### (No. 14.)

I, John Brailsford, of lawful age, testify that on Monday evening, the 5th instant, as I was passing by the sentry at Col. Dalrymple's house in Greene's lane, I asked a soldier named Swan, of the 29th regiment, what was the reason of their people's going about armed with clubs in such a manner, and troubling the town's people. Swan told me, " You will see, you had better go home," and more to the same purpose. When the guns were fired, I returned back and asked Swan what that could mean ? Swan, waving his head, said, " It's the guards ; there is no shot there ; you had better go home ;" and by all his behaviour and discourse he manifested his full acquaintance with the whole affair.—And further saith not.

JOHN BRAILSFORD.

Suffolk, ss. Boston, March 21, 1770. John Brailsford, above-named, after due examination, made oath to the truth of the above-written affidavit, taken to perpetuate the remembrance of the thing.
Before JOHN RUDDOCK, Just. Peace and the Quorum,
JOHN HILL, Just. Peace.

---

### (No. 15.)

Nathaniel Noyes, of lawful age, testifies and says, that on last Sabbath evening, the 4th day of March current, a little after dark, he saw five or six soldiers of the 14th and 29th regiments, each of them with clubs, passing through Fore street, and heard them say, that if they saw any of the inhabitants of this town out in the street after nine o'clock, they swore by God, they would knock them down, be they who they will.    NATH. NOYES.

Suffolk, ss.   Boston, March 16, 1770.   Nathaniel Noyes, above-named, after due examination, made oath to the truth of the above-written affidavit, taken to perpetuate the remembrance of the thing.

Before RI. DANA, Just. of Peace and of the Quorum.
JOHN HILL, Just. Peace.

---

(No. 16.)

Richard Ward, of lawful age, does testify and say, that on the Lord's day evening preceding the fifth day of March instant, about dusk, he went to see one Mr. Dines (who is a soldier in the 29th regiment, and who worked, when he was not upon duty, in Mr. John Piemont, peruke maker's shop, with the deponent, a journeyman to said Piemont) ; the said Dines lives near the barracks at New Boston ; when your deponent was there, he heard one of the officers of the said 29th regiment say to the sergeants, " Don't let any of your people go out unless there be eight or ten together."

RICHARD WARD.

Suffolk, ss.   Boston, March 16, 1770.   Richard Ward, above-named, after due examination, made oath to the truth of the above-written affidavit, taken to perpetuate the remembrance of the thing.

Before RI. DANA, Just. of Peace and of the Quorum.
JOHN HILL, Just. Peace.

---

(No 17.)

Jane Usher, of lawful age, testifies and says, that about nine o'clock in the morning of Monday the fifth day of March current, she being in the front chamber of the house of John Scollay, Esq., on Dock square, from the window saw two persons in the habit of soldiers, one of whom being on horseback, appeared to be an officer's servant.   The person on the horse first spoke to the other, but what he said she is not able to say, though the window was open, and she not more than twenty feet distant ; the other replied, " He hoped he should see blood enough spilt before morning."

JANE USHER.

Suffolk, ss.   Boston, March 16, 1770.   Jane Usher, above-named, after due examination, made oath to the truth of the above-written affidavit, taken to perpetuate the remembrance of the thing.

Before RI. DANA, Just. of Peace and of the Quorum.
JOHN HILL, Just. Peace.

(No. 18.)

Matthew Adams (living with Mr. John Arnold) being of lawful
age, testifies and says, that on Monday evening the fifth day of
March instant, between the hours of seven and eight of the clock, he
went to the house of Corporal Pershall, of the twenty-ninth regiment, near Quaker lane, where he saw the corporal and his wife,
with one of the fifers of said regiment; when he had got what
he went for, and was coming away, the corporal called him back,
and desired him with great earnestness to go home to his master s
house as soon as business was over, and not to be abroad on any account that night in particular, for the soldiers were determined to
be revenged on the ropewalk people ; and that much mischief would
be done ; upon which the fifer (about eighteen or nineteen years of
age), said he hoped in God they would burn the town down ; on
this he left the house, and the said corporal called after him again,
and begged he would mind what he had said to him ; and further
saith not.                                        MATTHEW ADAMS.

  Suffolk, ss.  Boston, March 20, 1770.  Matthew Adams, above-
        named, after due examination, made oath to the truth of
        the aforesaid affidavit, taken to perpetuate the remem-
        brance of the thing.
  Before JOHN RUDDOCK, Just. Peace and of the Quorum.
        JOHN HILL, Just. Peace.

(No. 19.)

Caleb Swan, of lawful age, testifies and says, that last Monday
night, the 5th of March 1770, being at Mr. Sample's door, at the
north part of the town, near the north battery, at the time of the
bells ringing for fire, he heard a woman's voice, whom he knew to
be the supposed wife of one Montgomery, a grenadier of the 29th
regiment, standing at her door, and heard her say it was not fire ;
the town was too haughty and too proud ; that many of their arses
would be laid low before the morning.  Upon which Susanna Cath-
cart said to her, I hope your husband will be killed.  On which the
woman replied, my husband is able and will stand his ground.
                                                  CALEB SWAN.

  Suffolk, ss.  Boston, March 21, 1770.  Caleb Swan, above-
        named, after due examination, made oath to the truth of
        the above affidavit, taken to perpetuate the remembrance
        of the thing.
  Before JOHN RUDDOCK, Just. Peace and of the Quorum.
        JOHN HILL, Just. Peace.

(No. 20.)

Margaret Swansborough, of lawful age, testifies and says, that
a free woman, named Black Peg, who has kept much with the
soldiers, on hearing the disturbance on Monday evening, the 5th

instant, said, " the soldiers were not to be trod upon by the inhabitants, but would know before morning, whether they or the inhabitants were to be masters." Since which time, the said Black Peg has sold off her household stuff and left the town, on her hearing what she had said before was given in to the committee of enquiry.

her<br>
MARGARET + SWANSBOROUGH,<br>
mark.

Suffolk, ss. Boston, March 20, 1770. Margaret Swansborough, aforenamed, after due examination, made oath to the truth of the aforesaid affidavit, taken to perpetuate the remembrance of the thing.

Before JOHN RUDDOCK, Just. Peace and of the Quorum.
BELCHER NOYES, Just. Peace.

(No. 21.)

Robert Pierpont, of lawful age, testifies and says, that going to see a sick neighbor between the hours of seven and eight on Monday evening, the fifth current, two soldiers armed, one with a broad sword, the other with a club, passed him near the hay market, going towards the town-house, seeming in great haste. In a few minutes they returned and hollowed very loud, " Colonel." Before the deponent reached Mr. West's house, where he was going, they passed him again, joined by another, with a blue surtout, who had a bayonet, with which he gave the deponent a back-handed stroke, apparently more to affront than hurt him. On complaint of this treatment, he said, the deponent should soon hear more of it, and threatened him very hard, and further saith not. ROB. PIERPONT.

Suffolk, ss. Boston, March 16, 1770. Robert Pierpont, above named, after due examination, made oath to the truth of the above written affidavit, taken to perpetuate the remembrance of the thing.

Before RI. DANA, Just. Peace and of the Quorum.
JOHN HILL, Just. Peace.

(No. 22.)

John Brown, of lawful age, testifies and says, that coming homewards about nine of the clock on Monday evening, the fifth current, he fell in with Nathaniel Bosworth, and walking slowly together, a little to the southward of Liberty-tree so called, they met a parcel of soldiers, about six or seven in number, walking very fast into town, one of the foremost said, " damn you stand out of the way," and struck the deponent a blow on the breast, which made him stagger and fall nearly to the ground, though he had sheared out of the way. The soldiers pressed along cursing and damning, towards the town-house with naked bayonets in their hands.

JOHN BROWN.

Suffolk, ss.  Boston, March 17, 1770.  John Brown, above-
named, after due examination, made oath to the truth of
the above affidavit, taken to perpetuate the remembrance
of the thing.

Before RI. DANA, Just. Peace and of the Quorum.

JOHN HILL, Just. Peace.

The following deposition should have immediately preceded No. 5.

(No. 23.)

Samuel Bostwick, of lawful age, testifies and says, that on Friday, the 2d instant, between ten and eleven o'clock in the forenoon,
three soldiers of the 29th regiment, came up Mr. Gray's ropewalk,
and William Green, one of the hands, spoke to one of them, saying,
" soldier, will you work ?"  The soldier replied, " yes."  Green said,
" then go and clean my s—t-house."  The soldier swore by the Holy
Ghost that he would have recompense, and tarried a good while
swearing at Green, who took no further notice of him, and then
went off, and soon after returned to the ropewalk with a party of
thirty or forty soldiers, headed by a tall negro drummer, and challenged the rope makers to come out.  All hands then present, being
about thirteen or fourteen, turned out and beat them off, considerably
bruised.  And further saith not.

SAMUEL BOSTWICK.

Suffolk, ss.  Boston, March 19, 1770.  Samuel Bostwick, above-
named, after due examination, made oath to the truth of
the above affidavit, taken to perpetuate the remembrance
of the thing.

Before RI. DANA, Just. of Peace and of the Quorum.

JOHN HILL, Just. Peace.

(No. 24.)

I, William Tyler, of lawful age, do testify and say, that on the
evening of the fifth of March, a little after nine o'clock, as I was
coming up King street, just before I got to the custom house, I saw
the sentinel running after a boy, and immediately heard him cry out
as though in great distress.  I asked the boy what was the matter ;
he told me the sentinel had struck him with his gun and bayonet because he asked Captain Goldfinch for some money that he owed him.
The sentinel said that he should not use an officer ill in the street.
Soon after the boy left the sentinel and went away, and immediately
ten or twelve soldiers came running up Silsby's alley, crying out,
" Where are your Sons of Liberty ?" and went from thence to Cornhill.  I further testify, that when the above complaint was made of
the sentinel's striking the barber's boy, there were few people in
the street.  I saw but five or six about them, who immediately
dispersed.  I then left King street, and went up to Cornhill.

WILLIAM TYLER.

Suffolk, ss. Boston, March 21, 1770. William Tyler, above
    named, after due examination, made oath to the truth of
    the aforesaid affidavit, taken to perpetuate the remem-
    brance of the thing.
Before, JOHN RUDDOCK, Just. Peace and of the Quorum,
    JOHN HILL, Just. Peace.

(No. 25.)

Henry Bass, of lawful age, testifies and says, that going from his
house in Winter-street, on Monday evening, the fifth of March, to
see a friend in the neighborhood of the Rev. Dr. Cooper's meeting-
house ; that the bell was ringing for nine o'clock when he came out
of his house, and that he proceeded down the Main street, and going
near Draper's alley, leading to Murray's barracks, through which he
purposed to pass, heard some boys huzzaing, and imagines that there
were six or seven of them and not more—and presently after he saw
two or three persons in said alley with weapons, but cannot positively say what they were.    Soon after several more came into the
alley and made a sally out, and those that came out were soldiers,
and thinks were all grenadiers, as they were stout men, and were
armed with large naked cutlasses ; they made at every body
coming in their way, cutting and slashing ; the said deponent very
narrowly escaped receiving a cut from the foremost of them, who
pursued him below Mr. Simpson's stone shop, where he made a
stand ; presently after, going up Cornhill, he met an oyster man,
who said to the deponent, " Damn it, this is what I got by going
up," and showed the deponent a large cut he had received from one
of the soldiers with a cutlass, over his right shoulder ; said deponent thinking it not safe but very dangerous for him to go through
the alley, he returned home by the way of King-street, through Royal
Exchange lane, and passed by the sentinel at the corner of the
Custom-house.    And said deponent further says, that he never saw
fewer persons in King street, considering the pleasantness of the
evening, and verily believes there was not twelve persons between
the Crown coffee-house and the bottom of the Town-house ; he
imagines it to be then about fifteen or twenty minutes after nine.
After said deponent got to the head of the Town-house, he met a
great many persons who enquired of him about the affair ; the said
deponent told them there had been an affray by Murray's barracks,
but that it was then over.    And further this deponent saith not.

                                                    HENRY BASS.
Suffolk, ss.   Boston, March 16, 1770.   The above-named Henry
    Bass personally appearing, and being carefully examined
    and duly cautioned to testify the whole truth, maketh
    solemn oath to the fore-written deposition by him sub-
    scribed, taken to perpetuate the remembrance of the thing.
Before, RI. DANA, Justice of the Peace and of the Quorum,
    JOHN HILL, Just. Peace.
    4

## (No. 26.)

I, William LeBaron, of Boston, of lawful age, testify and say, that on Monday evening the fifth day of this instant March, about ten minutes after nine o'clock, being in King street with my brother Francis LeBaron, saw a soldier, the sentry of the Custom-house door, running after a barber's boy; the boy called out as if he was in distress, and the soldier pursuing him with his firelock, tol<sup>d</sup> him if he did not hold his tongue he would put a ball through him, after which the soldier returned to his post; immediately after this I heard a great noise in Silsby's lane, so called, and immediately about thirteen or fourteen soldiers appeared in King street, near the watch-house, with their drawn swords, cutlasses, and bayonets, calling out, " Where are the damned boogers, cowards, where are your Liberty boys ;" at which time there was not more than eight or ten persons in King street; one of the soldiers came up to me, damned me, and made several passes at me with a drawn sword, the last of which the sword went between my arm and breast, and then I run, as I had nothing to defend myself, and was pursued by a soldier with a naked bayonet, who swore he would run me through ; at which time your deponent cried fire ! and soon after the bells rung, and further your deponent saith not.          WILLIAM LEBARON.

Suffolk, ss.   Boston, March 19, 1770.   William LeBaron, above-named, after due examination, made oath to the truth of the above-written affidavit, taken to perpetuate the remembrance of the thing.

Before, RI. DANA, Justice of Peace and of the Quorum,
JOHN HILL, Just. Peace.

---

## (No. 27.)

William Lewis, testifies and says, that on the evening following Monday the fifth instant, about nine o'clock, he passing through King street, in order to go into Cornhill street, while he was crossing King street heard some people wrangling at the Custom-house door, and he immediately saw four soldiers of the 29th regiment jump out from between the Watch-house and the Town-house steps, at the east end of the house, in their short jackets with drawn swords in their hands, two of whom run after the deponent and pursued him close until he got to his home in Cornhill street, where just as he entered the door one of the soldiers struck at him either with his sword or bayonet, but the deponent rather thinks it was the latter, as he afterwards found a three-square hole cut in the skirt of his surtout, which he verily believes was made by the blow that the soldier struck at him ; and further saith not.          WILLIAM LEWIS.

Suffolk, ss.   Boston, March 20, 1770.   William Lewis, above-named, after due examination, made oath to the truth of the above affidavit, taken to perpetuate the remembrance of the thing.

Before, JOHN RUDDOCK, Justice of Peace and of the Quorum,
JOHN HILL, Just. Peace.

(No. 28.)

Nathaniel Thayer, of lawful age, testifies, that on Monday evening the 5th of March, about nine of the clock, as he sat in his house in Cornhill he heard a great noise, at which he went to the door, and saw a number of people by Mr. Quincy's door, near Murray's barracks, where he heard the sticks and clubs going, upon which fire was cried, and presently ran five soldiers as he supposes from the main-guard, with swords or cutlasses, swearing and damning, and saying, " Where are they ? cut them to pieces." The soldiers in their waistcoats came to his door and insulted him ; so he shut his door and went in. NATH. THAYER.

Suffolk, ss. Boston, March 19, 1770. Nathaniel Thayer, above-named, after due examination, made oath to the truth of the above affidavit, taken to perpetuate the remembrance of the thing.

Before, RI. DANA, Justice of Peace and of the Quorum,
JOHN HILL, Just. Peace.

———

(No. 29.)

I, Isaac Parker, of lawful age, testify and say, that being at Mr. Richard Salter's house on the evening of the fifth current, heard a great noise in the street, upon which I went to the entry door and saw a great number of soldiers in their jackets without sleeves, having naked cutlasses in their hands, flourishing them over their heads, one of whom assaulted me with a naked cutlass, aiming a stroke at my head, which I happily avoided by a sudden retreat in-doors.
ISAAC PARKER.

Suffolk, ss. Boston, March 19, 1770. Isaac Parker, above-named, after due examination, made oath to the truth of the above-written affidavit, taken to perpetuate the remembrance of the thing.

Before, RI. DANA, Just. of Peace and of the Quorum,
JOHN HILL, Just. Peace.

———

(No. 30.)

I, Bartholomew Kneeland, of Boston, merchant, being of lawful age, testify and say, that on Monday evening, the fifth instant (being at my lodgings at the house of my sister, Mrs. Mehetable Torrey, widow of the late Mr. Samuel Torrey, deceased), about fifteen minutes after nine o'clock, hearing a bell ring, which I supposed was for fire, went immediately to the front door, followed by Mr. Matthias King, Mrs. Torrey, and two others of the family ; standing at the door for the space of four or minutes, I saw a number of soldiers, with broadswords and bayonets, in the main street near the town pump, making a great noise. One of the said soldiers, when nearly opposite to me, spake to me the following words, viz., " Damn you, what do you do there ? Get in." To which I made no answer. The same soldier immediately crossed the gutter, and, coming up to me, pointed his naked bayonet within six inches of my breast; I told him to go along, and then I retired into the house. In about half an hour's time after the above, I heard a volley of small arms fired off in King street; and upon inquiry was told that three men were killed and one wounded.

BART. KNEELAND.

Suffolk, ss. Boston, March, 12, 1770. Bartholomew Kneeland, above-named, after due examination, made oath to the above-written affidavit, taken to perpetuate the remembrance of the thing.

Before, RI. DANA, Just. of Peace and of the Quorum,
JOHN HILL, Just. Peace.

(No. 31.)

I, Nathaniel Appleton, of lawful age, testify, that on Monday evening, the 5th instant, between nine and ten o'clock, I was sitting in my house in Cornhill, heard a noise in the street, I went to my front door and saw several persons passing up and down the street; I asked what was the matter? was informed that the soldiers at Murray's barrack were quarrelling with the inhabitants. Standing there a few minutes, I saw a number of soldiers, about twelve or fifteen, as near as I could judge, come down from the southward, running toward the said barrack with drawn cutlasses, and appeared to be passing by, but on seeing me in company with Deacon Marsh at my door, they turned out of their course and rushed upon us with uplifted weapons, without our speaking or doing the least thing to provoke them; with the utmost difficulty we escaped a stroke by retreating and closing the door upon them.

I further declare, that at that time my son, a lad about twelve years old, was abroad on an errand, and soon came home and told me that he was met by a number of soldiers with cutlasses in their hands, one of which attempting to strike him, the child begged for his life, saying, " Pray soldier, save my life ;" on which the soldier replied, " No, damn you, I will kill you all," and smote him with his cutlass, which glanced down along his arm and knocked him to the ground, where they left him. After the soldiers had all passed, the child arose and came home, having happily received no other damage than a bruise on the arm. I further declare that the above-related transactions happened but a few minutes before the soldiers fired upon the people in King street; and further saith not.

NATH. APPLETON.

Suffolk, ss. Boston, March 20, 1770. Nathaniel Appleton, above-named, after due examination, made oath to the truth of the above affidavit, taken to perpetuate the remembrance of the thing.

Before, JOHN RUDDOCK, Just. Peace, and the Quorum,
JOHN HILL, Just. Peace.

(No. 32.)

Jeremiah Belknap, of lawful age, testifies and says, that on the first appearance of the affray in Cornhill on Monday evening, the fifth instant, hearing a noise he ran to his door and heard Mr. William Merchant say he had been struck by a soldier, and presently saw to the number of eight or nine soldiers come out of Boylston's alley into the street, armed with clubs and cutlasses. The deponent went into the street and desired them to retire to their barracks; upon which one of them, with a club in one hand and a cutlass in the other, with the latter made a stroke at the deponent; when finding there was no prospect of stopping them, the deponent ran to the main-guard, and called for the officers of the guard. The reply was, " There is no officer here." Several of the soldiers came out of the guard-house, and the deponent told them if there was not a party sent down there would be bloodshed. Just as the deponent spoke these words he was attacked by two soldiers, with drawn cutlasses, supposed of the party from Murray's barracks, one at his breast and the other over his head. One of the guards said, " This is an officer," meaning the deponent, I believe a constable; on which the two assailants retired and put up their cutlasses; and further saith not. JEREMIAH BELKNAP.

Suffolk, ss. Boston, March 16, 1770. The above-named Jeremiah Belknap, personally appeared, and being carefully examined, and duly cautioned to testify the whole truth, maketh solemn oath to the forewritten deposition by him subscribed, taken to perpetuate the remembrance of the thing.

Before, RI. DANA, Just. of Peace and of the Quorum,
JOHN HILL, Just. of Peace.

(No. 33.)

I, John Coburn, of lawful age, testify and say, that on the evening of the 5th of March instant, being alarmed by the cry of fire and ringing of bells, ran out of my house with my bags and buckets; upon going to Mr. Payne's door, he told me it was not fire, it was a riot. I sent my buckets home again, and went to Mr. Amory's corner with Mr. Payne, and Mr. Walker, the builder, came along and said the soldiers were in the street in Cornhill and Dock-square, with their drawn cutlasses, cutting and slashing every body in their way, and the inhabitants wanted help, and said, pray gentlemen run, or words to that purpose. I returned again to my house, and a few minutes after, at the head of Royal Exchange lane, in the street, I saw a few, not exceeding fifteen or twenty persons, stop, as I supposed, talking what had happened. I went to Mr. Payne's door and stood in his entry with him, I believe, about ten or fifteen minutes, and heard some words with the people and the sentinel, such as, Do fire if you dare, but no further than words, not so much as to touch him, as I saw; neither did I see more than five or six that had so much as sticks in their hands, all entirely unarmed, without any weapons. Mr. Harrison Gray, jun., came into the entry to us, and upon this immediately came an officer with a party of six or seven men with their guns breast-high, and cleared the way, and by their behavior I did not know but they would fire. I said it was not prudent to tarry there ; went directly into my own house and called all my family in. To the best of my judgment, there was not more than fifty or sixty people in the street when the party came, and I believe it was not exceeding two minutes from the time that I left Mr. Payne to the firing of the guns, and further your deponent saith not.                                    JOHN COBURN.

Suffolk, ss.   Boston, March 16, 1770.   The above-named John
        Coburn, personally appearing, and being carefully examin-
        ed and duly cautioned to testify the whole truth, maketh
        solemn oath to the afore-written deposition by him sub-
        scribed, taken to perpetuate the remembrance of the
        thing.
Before, RI. DANA, Just. of Peace and of the Quorum,
        JOHN HILL, Just. Peace.

-----

### (No. 34.)

I, Robert Polley, of lawful age, testify and declare, that on Monday evening, the 5th inst., as I was going home, observed about ten persons standing near Mr. Taylor's door. After standing there a small space of time, I went with them towards Boylston's alley, opposite to Murray's barracks. We met in the alley about eight or nine soldiers, some of whom were armed with drawn swords and cutlasses, one had a tongs, another a shovel, with which they assaulted us, and gave us a great deal of abusive language. We then drove them back to the barracks with sticks only ; we looked for stones or bricks but could find none, the ground being covered with snow. Some of the lads dispersed, and myself with a few others were returning peaceably home, when we met about nine or ten other soldiers armed with a naked cutlass in one hand and a stick or bludgeon in the other. One of them said, " Where are the sons of bitches ?" They struck at several persons in the street, and went towards the head of the alley. Two officers came and endeavored to get them into the barracks. One of the lads proposed to ring the bell. The soldiers went through the alley, and the boys huzzaed and said they were gone through Royal Exchange lane into King street. Myself and some of the boys then went into King street. I saw two or three snow balls strike the side of the Custom House, near which a sentinel stood. The sentinel kept the boys off with his bayonet charged breast high, which he frequently pushed at them. I then saw eight or nine soldiers with a leader come from the main guard towards the Custom House, where they drew up, three facing up the street and three fronting the street. They kept continually striking and pushing with their bayonets at the people who pressed towards them, without offering any insult as I saw. I then went down Royal Exchange lane. When I was in the middle of the lane I heard the discharge of a gun, which was immediately followed by about seven others. And further saith not.

his<br>
ROBERT + POLLEY,<br>
mark.

Attest. WM. PALFREY.

Suffolk, ss. Boston, March 17, 1770. Robert Polley, above-named, after due examination, made oath to the truth of the above affidavit, taken to perpetuate the remembrance of the thing.

Before, RI. DANA, Justice of Peace and of the Quorum,
JOHN HILL, Justice Peace.

---

### (No. 35.)

Samuel Atwood, of Welfleet, of lawful age, testifies and says, that a few minutes after nine of the clock on Monday evening last, lying on board a vessel in the town dock, he heard a noise and disturbance at the upper end of Dock Square, and going up he found the soldiers and inhabitants engaged in the narrow passes round Murray's barracks so called; the latter being mostly boys unarmed, dispersed, on which ten or twelve soldiers armed with drawn cutlasses, clubs, and bayonets bolted out of the alley into the square and met the deponent, who asked them if they intended to murder people? They answered, "Yes, by God, root and branch," saying, "here is one of them;" with that one of them struck the deponent with a club, which was repeated by another: the deponent being unarmed turned to go off, and he received a wound on the left shoulder, which reached the bone, disabled him, and gave him much pain. Having gone a few steps, the deponent met two officers, and asked them, gentlemen, what is the matter? They answered, "You will see by and by;" and as he passed by Colonel Jackson's, he heard the cry, "Turn out the guards."

SAMUEL ATWOOD.

Suffolk, ss. March 16, 1770. The above-named, Samuel Atwood, appeared before us, two of his Majesty's Justices of the Peace for the said county of Suffolk, and being carefully examined, and duly cautioned to declare the whole truth, made oath to the truth of the above testimony by him subscribed, taken to perpetuate the remembrance of the thing.

Before, RI. DANA, Justice of Peace and of the Quorum,
JOHN HILL, Justice Peace.

---

### (No. 36.)

Captain James Kirkwood, of lawful age, testifies and says, that about nine of the clock in the evening of the fifth day of March current, he was going by Murray's barracks, hearing a noise, stopped at Mr. Rhoads's door, opposite to said barracks, where said Rhoads was standing, and stood some time and saw the soldiers coming out of the yard from the barracks, armed with cutlasses and bayonets, and rushing through Boylston's alley into Cornhill. Two officers, viz., Lieuts. Minchin and Dickson, came out of the mess-house and said to the soldiers, my lads come into the barrack and don't hurt the inhabitants, and then retired into the mess-house. Soon after they came to the door again, and found the soldiers in the yard; and directly upon it, Ensign Mall came to the gate of the barrack yard, and said to the soldiers, " Turn out, and I will stand by you !" This he repeated frequently, adding, " Kill them ! stick them! knock them down, run your bayonets through them," with a great deal of language of like import. Upon which a great number of soldiers came out of the barracks, with naked cutlasses, headed by said Mall, and went through the aforesaid alley, some officers came and got the soldiers into their barracks ; and that Mall, with his sword or cutlass drawn in his hand, as often had them out again ; but they were at last drove into their barracks by the aforesaid Minchin and Dickson.           JAMES KIRKWOOD.

Suffolk, ss.   Boston, March 21, 1770.   James Kirkwood, above-named, after due examination, made oath to the truth of the aforesaid affidavit, taken to perpetuate the remembrance of the thing.

Before, JOHN RUDDOCK, Justice of Peace and of the Quorum, And, JOHN HILL, Justice Peace.

------

(No. 37.)

Matthias King, of Halifax, in Nova Scotia, of lawful age, testifies and says, that in the evening of the fifth day of March instant, about nine of the clock, he was at his lodgings at Mrs. Torrey's, near the town pump, and heard the bells ring and the cry of fire ; upon which he went to the door, and saw several soldiers coming round the south side of the town house armed with bayonets, and something which he took to be broad-swords ; that one of those people came up almost to him and Mr. Bartholomew Kneeland ; and they had but just time to shut the door upon him, otherwise he is well assured they must have fell victims to their boundless cruelty : He afterwards went into the upper chamber of the said house, and was looking out of the window when the drum and the guard went to the barrack ; and he saw one of the guards kneel and present his piece with a bayonet fixed, and heard him sware he would fire upon a parcel of boys who were then in the street, but he did not. He further declares, that when the body of troops was drawn up before the guard-house (which was presently after the massacre), he heard an officer say to another, that this was fine work, and just what he wanted ; but in the hurry he could not see him, so as to know him again.           MATTHIAS KING.

Suffolk, ss. Boston, March 17, 1770. Matthias King, above named, after due examination, made oath to the truth of the above affidavit, taken to perpetuate the remembrance of the thing.

Before, R<small>t.</small> D<small>ANA</small>, Just. of Peace and of the Quorum,
J<small>OHN</small> H<small>ILL</small>, Just. of Peace.

---

(No. 38.)

Bartholomew Broaders, of lawful age, testifies and says, that on Sunday evening, being the 4th instant, preceding the massacre, he went up to see Patrick Dines, a soldier of the 29th regiment, who worked with Mr. Piemont, and in Dawson's room heard Sergeant Daniels say, that the officers said, since patience would not do, force must. And that the soldiers must not bear the affronts of the inhabitants any longer, but resent them, and make them know their distance ; and further, that the inhabitants would never be easy, and that he should desire to make the plumbs fly about their ears, and set the town on fire round them, and then they would know who and who were of a side—said Daniels asked Edward Garrick, fellow-apprentice to the deponent, if he knew where he could get a stick that would bear a good stroke ? Garrick replied, you must look for one. And the deponent further saith, that about eight o'clock on Monday evening, he went down King street, and met twelve of the towns people with clubs, who said that they had been attacked by the soldiers ; that he followed the towns people to the conduit, and then returned home. Soon after Mr. Green's maid and his daughter called him out of the shop, and asked him to go to the apothecaries ; and then they with the deponent returned to the custom-house ; in going he met his fellow-apprentice, and they went and stood upon the Custom-house steps, and Mr. Hammond Green came out, saying, come in girls ; then the deponent and his fellow-apprentice, by the maid's invitation, went in also. Soon after Sawny Irving, so called, came in as he thought without a hat, seemed a little angry, and he thinks asked for a candle, (the maid has since told him he did ask for one), then he went through the room along with Hammond Green, the latter returned into the kitchen, then he left the house and went home ; after which the deponent came down King street, and went through Quaker lane, and coming up the lane again, saw the sentinel at the Custom-house leave his post and come into the middle of the street, and said to the deponent's fellow-apprentice, —who he thought had said something of an officer's not paying his debts—let me see your face ; the boy answered, I am not ashamed to show my face ; immediately upon which the sentinel fetched a sweeping stroke with his gun, upon the side of his head, which made him reel and stagger about, and cry much. The deponent asked what he was struck for ; he answered for nothing, he then asked the sentinel what he meant by thus abusing the people. He replied, damn your blood, if you do not get out of the way, I will give you something ; he then fixed his bayonet, and pushed at them, and they both run.  Then one Richard Ward, another fellow-apprentice, asked the one struck, what it was for, and endeavored to get his stick to strike the sentinel, but he told him not to, and came away ; then he heard a huzza or two, and as he got up Silsby's alley, up came a number of grenadiers, as he thought about ten, with clubs, cutlasses, and bayonets, crying out, where are the damned Yankees.  He replied, what is the matter, they answered, we will let you know.  He then run into his master's entry, and as running in, saw near twenty other soldiers with bayonets, &c. flourishing, coming from the guard house as he thought ; immediately after, he heard the bells ring, and then as he took it, the same party with a sergeant at their head, came running by, knocking down and slashing all the towns people they met with ; then he heard people who were running, ask where the fire was.  He told them it was no fire, but the soldier's near Justice Quincey's were fighting with the inhabitants.  He then went towards Justice Quincey's, and found the soldiers had retired to their barracks, when three cheers were given by the inhabitants.  He then went down to King street, and heard the people talking of the abuse his fellow-apprentices had received from the sentinel, but saw no insult offered the sentinel, the people being in the middle of the street.  One came up with a cane, appeared a gentleman, and spoke to the sentinel, and then went away ; then the sentinel went up the steps of the custom-house and pointed his gun ; some of the inhabitants then said he is going to fire—then he took down his gun and loaded it ; while he was loading, one Thomas Greenwood a waiter, went into the custom-house door, and it was shut immediately ; and then Mr. Green's son, John, said the sentinel was a going to fire ; but he saw no abuse offered him, or any danger he was in.  He then went down Royal Exchange lane, met a number of people who were also dispersing near Dock square.  He then said to one Cox and the people, that the soldiers were going to fire upon the inhabitants at the commissioner's steps ; some of the people went up upon this news to King street ; another man came from King street, and said to them, come up into King street.  He then went up Silsby's alley, and when he got to Mrs. Eustis's shop, heard a gun go off, and afterwards several others in a short space of time after one another.  Soon after he was told that three men were killed ; then heard the bells ring, and saw the people assemble fast in King street.  The deponent further saith, that on the night abovesaid, the snow was deep upon the ground, and well remembers that when the sentry called for the main guard, there were not above ten or twenty people in King street near the custom-house. And further saith not.

BARTHOLOMEW BROADERS.

Suffolk, ss.  Boston, March 19, 1770.  Bartholomew Broaders, above named, after due examination, made oath to the truth of the above-written affidavit, taken to perpetuate the remembrance of the thing.

Before, Ri. DANA, Just. of Peace and of the Quorum,
And, JOHN HILL, Just. Peace.

---

### (No. 39.)

John Goddard, of Brookline, testifies and says, as he was passing the street on Saturday last, being the 3d instant, he stopped near the barracks in Water street, and sold several of the barrack people some potatoes about five o'clock in the afternoon, and found by their discourse some of the soldiers had returned from a fray near the ropewalks, and a number of soldiers came out of the barracks, he supposed about twenty, with clubs, seemingly much enraged; and one in a profane manner swore he would be revenged on them, if he fired the town.                                         JOHN GODDARD.

Suffolk, ss.  Boston, March 22, 1770.  John Goddard, above-mentioned, after due examination made oath to the truth of the aforesaid affidavit, taken to perpetuate the remembrance of the thing.

Before, JOHN RUDDOCK, Just. Peace and of the Quorum,
And, JOHN HILL, Just. Peace.

---

### (No. 40.)

Daniel Calfe, of lawful age, testifies and says, that on Saturday evening, the 3rd instant, a camp woman, wife to James McDeed, a grenadier in the 29th, came into Daniel Calfe's shop, father to the deponent, and the people, talking about the affray at the ropework, and blaming the soldiers for the part they had acted in it.  The woman said the soldiers were in the right, adding that before Tuesday or Wednesday night they would wet their swords or bayonets in New England people's blood.  The deponent further says, that on the evening of the 5th current, hearing the bells ring, which he took for fire, he went out, and near the old south meeting house heard the soldiers were fighting with the inhabitants in King street, whereupon he came into King street, and seeing a number of people (about one hundred) he went up to the Custom House, where were posted about a dozen soldiers with an officer.  That this deponent heard said officer order the soldiers to fire, and gave the second word to fire before they fired ; and upon the officers ordering the soldiers to fire the second time, this deponent ran off about thirty feet distant, when turning about, he saw one Caldwell fall, and likewise a mulatto man.                                         DANIEL CALFE.

Suffolk, ss.  Boston, March 21, 1770.  Daniel Calfe, above named, after due examination, made oath to the truth of the aforesaid affidavit, taken to perpetuate the remembrance of the thing.

Before, JOHN RUDDOCK, Just. Peace and of the Quorum,
And, JOHN HILL, Just. Peace.

(No. 41.)

I, Thomas Marshall, of lawful age, do testify and declare, that, on Monday night, the 5th of March, four or five minutes after nine o'clock, coming from Col. Jackson's house on Dock Square, to my house in King street, next door to the Custom House, I saw no person in the street but the sentinel at the Custom House, in perfect peace. After I had been in my house ten or twelve minutes, being in my shop in the front of the house, I heard the cry of murder at a distance, on which I opened the door, but saw no person in the street; but in half a minute I saw several persons rushing out from the main guard house, crying out, damn them, where are they? They came down as far as the corner of Mr. Philips's house; I saw their swords and bayonets glitter in the moonlight, crying out as before, and by Jesus let them come; at which time I was called into the house by one of my family, but returned again in half a minute, and saw ten or twelve soldiers, in a tumultuous manner, in the middle of King street, opposite to Royal Exchange lane, flourishing their arms, and saying, damn them where are they, and crying fire; the bells then rung as for fire; I was then called in again for half a minute, and returning again to the door, the inhabitants began to collect. Soon after a party of soldiers came down the south side of King street and crossed over to the Custom House sentinel, and formed in a rank by him, nor did I see any manner of abuse offered the sentinel, and in three minutes at the farthest they began to fire on the inhabitants, by which several persons were killed, and several others were wounded. Some time after this, the party marched off very leisurely, and without molestation, and presently after the main guard was drawn out in ranks between the guard-house and town-house, and was joined by the piquet in the same manner, with fixed bayonets and muskets shouldered, except the front rank, who stood with charged bayonets, until the Lieutenant Governor came up. And I do further declare, as near as I can judge, there was not more than 100 persons in the street at the time the guns were discharged.                THO. MARSHALL.

Suffolk, ss.   Boston, March 20, 1770.   Thomas Marshall, Esq., above named, after due examination, made oath to the truth of the afore-written affidavit, taken to perpetuate the remembrance of the thing.

Before, RI. DANA, Just. Peace and of the Quorum,
SAM. PEMBERTON, Just. Peace.

(No. 42.)

I, John Leach, jun., of lawful age, do testify and say, that on Monday night, between the hours of nine and ten in the evening of the 5th instant, three youths and myself were passing through the alley leading from Justice Quincey's to Murray's barracks (so called); when we had got about half way through the alley a soldier of the 29th regiment with a dirty looking man overtook us, the soldier being armed with a cutlass or sword, and the man with a short thick club, and rushing through us, one of the youths asked what the matter was ; by that the man that had the club struck one of the youths on the shoulder; another of the youths asked him what he meant, by that the soldier came up and struck the youth with his sword or cutlass on his arm, which did him considerable damage ; then we all ran up the alley and asked for assistance, when soon came up some more soldiers out of their barracks through the alley armed with cutlasses, swords, shovels, and tongs, cutting and slashing, that we were obliged to run up the alley and stand at the head of the alley and keep them in as long as we could; but there were so many that we were obliged to run; but they immediately made after us and knocked several of us down, myself for one. Some time after two officers of the 29th regiment came up the alley and drove the soldiers home to their barracks, and then the people chiefly dispersed, myself for one ; as I was going down Dock square to go home I heard a number of people hallow, Run up King street, for the soldiers are knocking people down ; after some time considering what the matter was, I ran up Royal Exchange alley, so called; when I had got to the head of the alley, I saw about eight soldiers standing round the sentry box by the Custom-House with their guns levelled breast high and a considerable number of people stand in King street; when I had been there about three minutes I heard the word fire (but who it came from I cannot say), but nobody seemed to mind it ; about half a minute after I heard the word fire again, and some other words, but could not tell what they were ; directly the soldier on the right hand fired, I had a blow on my back which I thought was from the butt of a gun, I was then a-going off when I heard five or six guns go off which I took to be nothing but powder at first, till I see two men drop, by this the people seemed to disperse, then I was going up by the Town House when I saw the people bringing along two dead men, a little while after the whole of the 29th regiment drew up by the Town House, I stayed a little while longer, and made the best of my way home. And further I say not. JOHN LEACH, JUN.

    Suffolk, ss. Boston, March 21, 1770. John Leach, Jun., above-named, after due examination, made oath to the truth of the aforesaid affidavit, taken to perpetuate the remembrance of the thing.
Before, JOHN RUDDOCK, Just. Peace and of the Quorum,
And, JOHN HILL, Just. Peace.

---

### (No. 43.)

    I, the subscriber, of lawful age, testify and say, that on Monday evening, the 5th instant, March 1770, being at the south part of the town between the hours of nine and ten o'clock, I heard the bells in the centre of the town ring, and fire cried, ran immediately for King street, where I supposed it was, and to my great astonish-

ment, I saw a number of soldiers with presented bayonets, commanded by an officer whom I did not then know; the soldiers formed a semi-circle round the sentinel box to the Custom-House door
—I went immediately up to them, and spoke to the fourth man
from the corner, who stood in the gutter, and asked him if the soldiers were loaded, he replied Yes! I then asked (addressing myself
to the whole), if they intended to fire, was answered positively, Yes,
by the Eternal God. I then looked round to see what number of
inhabitants were in the street, and computed them to be about fifty,
who were then going off as fast as possible; at the same time I observed a tall man standing on my left-hand, who seemed not apprehensive of the danger he was in, and before I had time to speak to
him, I heard the word " Fire!" and immediately the report followed, the man on my left hand dropped, I asked him if he was hurt,
but received no answer, I then stooped down and saw him gasping
and struggling with death. I then saw another man laying dead on
my right-hand, but further advanced up the street. I then saw the
soldiers loading again, and I ran up the street to get some assistance
to carry off the dead and wounded. Doctor Jos. Gardner, and
David Bradley, came down with me to the corpses, and as we were
stooping to take them up, the soldiers presented at us again; I then
saw an officer passing busily behind them. We carried off the dead
without regarding the soldiers. I then saw an officer pass before
the soldiers and hove up their arms, and said stop firing, don't fire
any more, upon which they shouldered. I then went close up to
them, and addressing myself to the whole, told them I came to see
some faces that I might be able to swear to another day—Capt.
Preston, who was the officer, turned round and answered (in a melancholy tone), " perhaps you may." After taking a view of each
man's face I left them. They soon after ran up to the main guard-
house. I have nothing farther to say.        BENJ. BURDICK, JUN.

    Suffolk, ss.   Boston, March 20, 1770.   Benjamin Burdick, Jun.,
        above-named, after due examination, made oath to the
        truth of the aforesaid affidavit, taken to perpetuate the re-
        membrance of the thing.
    Before, JOHN RUDDOCK, Justice of Peace and of the Quorum,
    And, JOHN HILL, Justice Peace.

### (No. 44.)

    I, Charles Hobby, of lawful age, testify and say, that on Monday
evening the 5th instant, between the hours of nine and ten o'clock,
being in my master's house, was alarmed with the cry of fire, I ran
down as far as the town-house, and then heard that the soldiers and
the inhabitants were fighting in the alley by Dr. Cooper's meeting-
house. I went through the alley, I there saw a number of soldiers
about the barracks, some with muskets, others without. I saw a
number of officers at the door of the mess-house, almost fronting the
alley, and some of the inhabitants intreating the officers to com-

mand the soldiers to be peaceable and retire to their barracks. One of the officers, viz., Lieut. Minchin, replied, that the soldiers had been abused lately by the inhabitants, and that if the inhabitants would disperse, the soldiers should follow their example. Captain Goldfinch was among the rest of the officers in or about the steps of the mess-house door, but did not command the soldiers. I then left them and went to King street. I then saw a party of soldiers loading their muskets about the Custom-house door, after which they all shouldered. I heard some of the inhabitants cry out, " heave no snow balls ;" others cried " they dare not fire." Capt. Preston was then standing by the soldiers, when a snow ball struck a grenadier, who immediately fired, Capt. Preston standing close by him. The Captain then spoke distinctly, " Fire, Fire !" I was then within four feet of Capt. Preston, and know him well ; the soldiers fired as fast as they could one after another. I saw the mulatto fall, and Mr. Samuel Gray went to look at him, one of the soldiers, at the distance of about four or five yards, pointed his piece directly for the said Gray's head and fired. Mr. Gray, after struggling, turned himself right round upon his heel and fell dead. Capt. Preston some time after ordered them to march to the guard-house. I then took up a round hat and followed the people that carried him down to a house near the post-office. And further saith not.

CHARLES HOBBY.

Suffolk, ss. Boston, March 20, 1770. Charles Hobby, above-named, after due examination, made oath to the truth of the aforesaid affidavit, taken to perpetuate the remembrance of the thing.

Before, JOHN RUDDOCK, Justice of Peace and of the Quorum, BELCHER NOYES, Justice of Peace.

(No. 45.)

I, William Tant, of lawful age, testify and say, that on Monday 5th instant, being then in a house on the Long Wharf, hearing a bell ring, imagined it was for fire : whereupon I run up King street, and inquiring the cause, was informed, that there had been a number of the inhabitants of the town insulted by the soldiers in different places. As I got abreast of Quaker lane, I met a number of persons, to the amount of thirty or forty, mostly boys and youngsters, who assembled in King street, before the Custom-house, and gave three cheers, and some of them being near the sentry, at the Custom-house door, damned him, and bid him fire and be damned ; and some snow balls were throwed, or other things : whereupon the sentry stepped on the steps of the Custom-house door, and loaded his piece, and struck the butt of it against the steps, presented it at the people several times : at length the people drawing nearer to him, he knocked at the Custom-house door, and I saw it opened about half-way. In the space of six or seven minutes, I saw a party of soldiers come from the main guard, and draw themselves up in a line from the corner of the Custom-house to the sentry-box; the people still continued in the street, crying, "Fire, fire, and be damned," and hove some more snow balls; whereupon I heard a musket go off, and in the space of two or three seconds, I heard the word fire given, but by whom I know not, and instantly the soldiers fired one after another. I then stood between the sentry-box and the Custom-house door. And further I know not.  WILLIAM TANT.

Suffolk, ss.  Boston, March 20, 1770. William Tant, above-named, after due examination, made oath to the truth of the aforesaid affidavit, taken to perpetuate the remembrance of the thing.

Before, JOHN RUDDOCK, Just. Peace and of the Quorum,
BELCHER NOYES, Justice o' Peace.

### (No. 46.)

I, Thomas Cain, of lawful age, testify and say, that on Monday, the 5th instant, being in a house on the long wharf, I heard a bell ring, which I imagined was for nine o'clock, but being informed by a person in my company that it was twelve minutes past that hour by his watch, I then concluded the bell rung for fire, so I ran up King street, in company with Mr. William Tant, and asking a few people whom I met the cause of the bell's ringing, was answered the soldiers had insulted some of the town's people by the ropewalks. I then went down Quaker lane as far as Justice Dana's house, where I met a number of people coming up, and asked them if there had been any disturbance at or near the ropewalks? They answered me, that there had been several people insulted and knocked down by the soldiers in different parts of the town. I then came up into King street, where they assembled together below the town house (to the best of my knowledge), between thirty and forty persons, mostly youngsters or boys, and when there they gave three cheers, and asked where the soldiers were (I imagine they meant them that had insulted them); some of the people assembled being near the sentry at the Custom House door, damn'd him, and I saw some snowballs or other things throwed that way, whereupon the sentry stepped on the steps at the Custom House door and loaded his piece, and when loaded struck the butt of his firelock against the steps three or four times, in the interim the people assembled, continuing crying "Fire, fire, and be damned," and some of them drawing near to him he knocked at the Custom House door very hard, whereupon the door was opened about halfway, and I saw a person come out, which I imagined to be a servant without a hat, his hair tied and hung down loose.

In the space of about five minutes, to the best of my remembrance, I perceived a party of soldiers come from the main-guard directly through the concourse of people that was then in King street, with their muskets and fixed bayonets, pushing to and fro, saying, "Make way;" when they had got abreast of the Custom house they drew up in a line from the corner of Royal Exchange lane to the sentry box at the Custom-house door, and being in that position for the space of five or six minutes, with their muskets levelled breast high and pointed at the people that was still in the street, huzzaing, &c., and crying fire, as before, and some more snowballs or other things being hove, I heard and saw the flash of a gun that went off near the corner of the afore-mentioned lane, and in the space of two seconds I heard the word " Fire" given, but by whom I cannot ascertain, but the soldiers fired regularly one after another, and when discharged, loaded again ; I then stood behind the sentry box, between the soldier next it and the Custom-house.

THOMAS CAIN.

Suffolk, ss. Boston, March 20, 1770. Thomas Cain, after due examination, made oath to the truth of the aforesaid affidavit, taken to perpetuate the remembrance of the thing.

Before, JOHN RUDDOCK, Just. Peace and of the Quorum,
BELCHER NOYES, Just. of Peace.

----

(No. 47.)

I, Peter Cunningham, of lawful age, testify, that on Monday evening, the 5th current, on the cry of fire, a few minutes after 9 o'clock, coming into King street, I saw Capt. Preston standing before the door where the main-guard was kept, and heard him say, " Turn out the guard !" Then I passed down King street, and saw the sentry at the Custom-house with his bayonet charged, dodging it about as if pushing at the boys, who seemed to be laughing at him, and none of them within twelve or fifteen feet of him. In a few minutes after, Captain Preston arrived with a party of soldiers, perhaps seven or eight, and took post between the Custom-house door and the west corner of said house, round the sentry box. As soon as they had taken their post, they began to push their bayonets at the people, though none seemed to offer them any offence. The captain quickly commanded them to prime and load, which being effected, they began to push as before. The captain came before them and put his arm under three or four of their pieces, and putting them into an upright posture, then retired from my sight ; and presently they again levelled and the firing began, and proceeded till ten or eleven pieces were discharged. On the people's scattering a little, I saw two men near me lay dead on the street, and observed the soldiers to load again, and moved off. And further I say not.

PETER CUNNINGHAM.

Suffolk, ss. Boston, March 20, 1770. Peter Cunningham, above-named, after due examination, made oath to the truth of the aforesaid affidavit. Taken to perpetuate the remembrance of the thing.

Before, JOHN RUDDOCK, Justice of Peace and Quorum,
JOHN HILL, Justice Peace.

5

(No. 48.)

I, Samuel Condon, of lawful age, testify and say, that on the night of the 5th instant March, being on the long wharf, between the hours of 9 and 10 o'clock, and hearing the bells ring as for fire, I ran up King street; on my coming nigh the town-house I saw a number of people, about thirty or forty, chiefly consisting of boys and lads, who proceeded down said street opposite the Custom-house ; the sentinel on their approach placed himself on the Custom-house steps, and charged his musket and presented the same against the body of the people who offered him no insult or violence ; in a few minutes after, a party came down from the main guard, consisting of about eight soldiers with their guns and bayonets in a charged position, headed by an officer, and posted themselves by the west corner of the Custom-house, round the sentry box in a half circle ; at this time I stood near the door of the Royal Exchange tavern, but apprehending danger as the soldiers stood with their muskets and bayonets in a charged or presented position, moved from thence down said Royal Exchange lane, and stood nigh the west end of the Custom-house ; during this interim I saw no violence offered the soldiers ; in a few minutes after having placed myself as aforesaid, a musket was fired by the soldier who stood next the corner, in a few seconds after another was fired, and so in succession till the whole was discharged, to the number of eight or thereabouts ; while the muskets were discharging I walked down the lane, and when the firing ceased I turned and went up to the head of the lane when I saw the people carrying off one dead person, and two more laying lifeless on the ground about two muskets' length from the said soldiers, inhumanly murdered by them, the blood then running from them in abundance ; a person asked the soldier who fired first, the reason for his so doing, the soldier answered, " Damn your bloods, you boogers, I would kill a thousand of you !" the soldiers were then charging their muskets again in order for a second discharge in case any insult had been offered them.     SAMUEL CONDON.

Suffolk, ss.   Boston, March 20, 1770.   Samuel Condon, above-named, after due examination, made oath to the truth of the aforesaid affidavit, taken to perpetuate the remembrance of the thing.

Before, JOHN RUDDOCK, Just. Peace and of the Quorum,
And, JOHN HILL, Just. Peace.

---

(No. 49.)

Ebenezer Hinckley, of Boston, of lawful age, declares, that on Monday evening the 5th of March current, that being at home in his house, he heard the bells ring, and came out, and came through Cornhill street, to the corner of King street, near the main-guard house ; immediately as he turned the corner, he saw a party of soldiers come out of the main-guard house, and he the deponent then saw an officer, as he thought, look out of the chamber window, and call to them, and said "Fire upon them, damn them, fire upon them." The deponent then followed them, viz., the said party of soldiers, to the place where they were posted, being before the sentry box in a half circle, near the Custom-house ; they reaching forward pushing their bayonets, and endeavoring to stab people, provoked a few boys to throw two or three snow-balls, and challenged them to fire. In about a minute after, the deponent heard the word "Fire," and then saw a stick thrown which hit a soldier's gun, whereupon the corner soldier fired, and the rest followed in the firing—when the firing was, the deponent verily believes there was not more than fifty or sixty persons in that part of the street—And it appeared to the deponent, that the soldiers going down to the Custom-house in so hostile a manner, was the occasion of drawing the most of those people there.—And the deponent further saith, that through the whole, he saw not one brick-bat or stone thrown, and believes that it was naturally impossible to come at any, as the snow was considerably deep.

*Memorandum.* After the party of soldiers were got to their place, he saw Capt. Preston who commanded them, whom he knew very well. And further saith not. EBENEZER HINCKLEY.

Suffolk, ₋ ss. Boston, March 20, 1770. Ebenezer Hinckley, above-named, after due examination, made oath to the truth of the above affidavit, taken to perpetuate the remembrance of the thing.

Before, JOHN RUDDOCK, Just. of Peace and of the Quorum,
And, JOHN HILL, Just. Peace.

----

(No. 50.)

Francis Archbald, jun., of lawful age, testifies and saith, that on Monday evening, the fifth of March instant, at about ten minutes past nine of the clock of said evening, as he was going through the alley that leads from Cornhill to Brattle street (so called), with several others with him, he saw a soldier with a cutlass, flourishing it about in said alley, and a mean-looking fellow with him, with a club in his hand ; then the deponent heard somebody outside of the alley speak to the said soldier, and told him to put up his cutlass, for it was not clever to carry such a weapon in the night without it was in the scabbard ; whereupon said soldier came up to him the deponent, with his cutlass pointing towards his breast, and damn'd him, and asked him what he had to say against it ; whereupon the deponent told him to stand off. The said soldier then went up to one of the lads that was with him and struck him (as the deponent thought), the deponent then went out of said alley and hollowed to some lads who were standing near the Town House ; when they came to deponent's assistance, they made said soldiers retire through said alley to the barracks ; in about five or six minutes after, about twelve or fifteen soldiers came out of said barracks (as I heard the next day they were encouraged and set on by Ensign Mall, belonging to the 29th

regiment), with cutlasses, tongs, and clubs, and came up to them
and damned them, and said, "Where is the Yankee boogers?"
when they began to strike the people in the street with said weapons. And as the deponent was standing with Mr. John Hicks, one
of the soldiers came up with a pair of tongs, and just going to make
a stroke at said deponent, said Hicks knocked him down, whereupon
the deponent, when said soldier got up, knocked him down again
and broke his wrist (as he was informed afterwards), then the deponent was going home to the south end. Just as he got to the
Town House he looked down King street and saw about fifty or
sixty people standing in the middle of said street, opposite the Custom-house, then the deponent went down to see what was the matter. When he got down said street he saw a party of soldiers coming from the main-guard (amongst which was one Matthew Kilroy,
of the 29th regiment), going to the sentinel that was standing at
the Custom-house. Then the deponent went over to the side of
the way and there stood about two minutes, when he saw the flash,
and heard the report of a gun that was fired from said sentinel's
post, and six or seven fired directly afterwards. Then the deponent
saw three men lying near said sentinel's post, dead. And the deponent further adds, that at the time of his standing there as aforesaid,
he saw nobody molest or trouble said sentinel or party of soldiers
(as aforesaid) in any shape whatever. And further the deponent
saith not.                                FRANCIS ARCHBALD, JUN.

Suffolk, ss.   Boston, March 17, 1770.   Francis Archbald, Jun.,
     above-named, after due examination, made oath to the
     truth of the above-written affidavit, taken to perpetuate
     the remembrance of the thing.
Before, RI. DANA, Just. of Peace and of the Quorum,
     JOHN HILL, Just. of Peace.

(No. 51.)

I, Nathaniel Fosdick, of lawful age, testify and say, that on the
night of the fifth instant, betwixt the hours of nine and ten
o'clock, being in my house with my family, hearing the bells ring
for fire ran out to assist the inhabitants, ran towards the north; when
I came to the Town House I see the people running down King
street, I followed; when I came by the guard-house I see some soldiers come out and fix their bayonets; I ran to know where the fire
was; after I had got into King street I made a halt, as I stopped I
was pushed behind, I turned round and saw some soldiers with their
bayonets charged, which came against me. I asked them if this was
the fire that is cried? They made no answer. I asked them what
they meant by coming on me in that manner? Their answer was,
"Damn you, stand out of our way." I told them I would not move
for no man under the heavens. I offended no one. Therefore they
passed me, some on my right and some on my left. I followed behind them; they went to the sentry box and faced round, and formed

in a half circle. I saw a number of people near the middle of King street, about twenty yards from the sentry box. I spoke out, and desired that no disturbance might be betwixt the inhabitants and the soldiers, for if the soldiers were in fault, there was their officer, which I looked upon to be the officer of the day, and he could settle the affair in one minute; then I spake to two men to speak to the officer; then I see two or three advance towards the officer. I heard some words pass, what they were I know not; I turned round and spake to the people to step off and let them that went to the officer settle the dispute; the people standing still, I turned towards the officer and see him fall into the regular circle, then I heard the word " Fire !" On my left one gun was fired off by a soldier on their right. Upon which I rushed in; then seeing the first soldier that fired run at some persons and fall upon the ground, I hollowed to take his gun from him, then I received three pushes by their bayonets, two in my left arm and one in my breast; that at my breast I struck off with a stick, and the gun went off instantly. Then I drew back, and finding one dead, as I thought, on my left and one on my right, I then run over to Quaker lane, where I saw a number of people, I desired them to step out and keep the soldiers from getting off; from thence I went over to the other side the street, to the lane near the town watch-house, where I desired the people to step out, and not to let the soldiers get off, for I would go home and get my gun and bring a party against them, which I did, but meeting some of the inhabitants returning, they told me the soldiers were gone off and affairs would be settled to-morrow, on that I went home. NATH. FOSDICK.

Suffolk, ss. Boston, March 17, 1770. Nath. Fosdick, above-named, after due examination, made oath to the truth of the above-written affidavit, taken to perpetuate the remembrance of the thing.

Before, RI. DANA, Just. of Peace and of the Quorum,
SAM. PEMBERTON, Just. of Peace.

---

(No. 52.)

Joseph Hooton, Jr., of lawful age, testifies and says, that coming from the south end of Boston, on Monday evening the fifth instant, against the old south meeting house, he heard a great noise and tumult, with the cry of murder often repeated. Proceeding towards the town-house the deponent passed by several soldiers running that way, with naked cutlasses and bayonets in their hands. The deponent asked one of them what was the matter, and was answered by him, " By God, you shall all know what is the matter soon !" Between nine and ten o'clock the deponent came into King street, and stood about the middle of the street, or nearer the Custom-house, in the direction of Quaker and Royal Exchange lanes, and saw about eight or ten soldiers drawn up near the Custom-house, and an officer, which he since understands was Capt. Preston, between the soldiers and the Custom-house. There was much noise and huzzaing among the boys and people, and some of the boys the deponent observed drew near to the soldiers. In this hurry and confusion, the deponent heard many ask each other whether they thought they would fire? and it was generally concluded they would not. But in about five minutes after the deponent first stood there, he heard the officer give the word " fire ;" they not then firing, he again said " fire," which they still disobeying, he said with a much higher voice, " Damn you, fire, be the consequence what it will!" Soon after this one of the guns went off—in a few seconds another, and so on, till six or seven were discharged. Near the deponent's left hand, dropt a man, which he since learns was Mr. James Caldwell, on which he left the place. And further saith not.

JOSEPH HOOTON, JR.

Suffolk, ss.   Boston, March 15, 1770.   The said Joseph Hooton, Jr., personally appearing, maketh solemn oath to the truth of the fore-written deposition, by him subscribed.

Before me, EDM. QUINCY, Just. Peace.

---

(No. 53.)

I, Richard Palmes, of Boston, of lawful age, testify and say, that between the hours of nine and ten o'clock of the fifth instant, I heard one of the bells ring, which I supposed was occasioned by fire, and enquiring where the fire was, was answered that the soldiers were abusing the inhabitants ; I asked where, was first answered at Murray's barracks. I went there and spoke to some officers that were standing at the door, I told them I was surprised they suffered the soldiers to go out of the barracks after eight o'clock ; I was answered by one of the officers, pray do you mean to teach us our duty ; I answered I did not, only to remind them of it. One of them then said, you see that the soldiers are all in their barracks, and why do you not go to your homes. Mr. James Lamb and I said, Gentlemen, let us go home, and were answered by some, home, home. Accordingly I asked Mr. William Hickling if he was going home, he said he was ; I walked with him as far as the post-office, upon my stopping to talk with two or three people, Mr. Hickling left me ; I then saw Mr. Pool Spear going towards the town-house, he asked me if I was going home, I told him I was ; I asked him where he was going that way, he said he was going to his brother David's. But when I got to the town-pump, we were told there was a rumpus at the Custom-house door ; Mr. Spear said to me you had better not go, I told him I would go and try to make peace. I immediately went there and saw Capt. Preston at the head of six or eight soldiers in a circular form, with guns breast high and bayonets fixed ; the said Captain stood almost to the end of their guns. I went immediately to Capt. Preston (as soon as Mr. Bliss had left him), and asked him if their guns were loaded, his answer was they are loaded with powder and ball ; I then said to him, I hope you do not intend they shall fire upon the inhabitants, his reply was, by no means. When I was asking him these questions, my left hand was on his right shoulder; Mr. John Hickling had that instant taken his hand off my shoulder, and stepped to my left, then instantly I saw a piece of snow or ice fall among the soldiers, on which the soldier at the officer's right hand stepped back and discharged his gun, at the space of some seconds the soldier at his left fired next, and the others one after the other. After the first gun was fired, I heard the word " fire," but who said it I know not. After the first gun was fired, the said officer had full time to forbid the other soldiers not to fire, but I did not hear him speak to them at all; then turning myself to the left I saw one man dead, distant about six feet; I having a stick in my hand made a stroke at the soldier who fired, and struck the gun out of his hand. I then made a stroke at the officer, my right foot slipped, that brought me on my knee, the blow falling short; he says I hit his arm; when I was recovering myself from the fall, I saw the soldier that fired the first gun endeavoring to push me through with his bayonet, on which I threw my stick at his head, the soldier starting back, gave me an opportunity to jump from him into Exchange lane, or I must been inevitably run through my body. I looked back and saw three persons laying on the ground, and perceiving a soldier stepping round the corner as I thought to shoot me, I ran down Exchange lane, and so up the next into King street, and followed Mr. Gridley with several other persons with the body of Capt. Morton's apprentice, up to the prison house, and saw he had a ball shot through his breast; at my return I found that the officers and soldiers were gone to the main guard. To my best observation there were not seventy people in King street at the time of their firing, and them very scattering; but in a few minutes after the firing there were upwards of a thousand. Finding the soldiers were gone I went up to the main-guard, and saw there the soldiers were formed into three divisions, the front division in the posture of platoon firing, and I expected they would fire. Hearing that his Honor the Lieutenant-Governor was going to the Council-chamber, I went there; his Honor looking out of the door desired the people to hear him speak, he desired them to go home and he would enquire into the affair in the morning, and that the law should take its course, and said, I will live and die by the law. A gentleman desired his Honor to order the soldiers to their barracks, he answered it was not in his power, and that he had no command over the troops, and that it lay with Col. Dalrymple and not with him, but that he would send for him, which after some time he did; upon that a gentleman desired his Honor to look out of the window facing the main-guard, to see the position the soldiers were in, ready to fire on the inhabitants, which he did after a good deal of persuasion, and called for Col. Carr and desired him to order the troops to their barracks in the same order they were in; accordingly they were ordered to shoulder their guns, and were marched off by some officers. And further saith not. RICH. PALMES.

Suffolk, ss. Boston, March 17, 1770. Richard Palmes, above-
named, after due examination, made oath to the truth of
the above affidavit, taken to perpetuate the remembrance
of the thing.

Before, Ri. DANA, Justice of Peace and of the Quorum,
JOHN HILL, Justice Peace.

---

(No. 54.)

I, William Wyat, of Salem, coaster, testify and say, that last
Monday evening, being the fifth day of March current, I was in Boston, down at Treat's wharf, where my vessel was lying, and hearing
the bells ring, supposed there was a fire in the town, whereupon I
hastened up to the Town-house, on the south side of it, where I saw an
officer of the army lead out of the guard-house there seven or eight
soldiers of the army, and lead them down in seeming haste, to the
Custom-house on the north side of King street, where I followed
them, and when the officer had got there with the men, he bid them
face about. I stood just below them on the left wing, and the said
officer ordered his men to load, which they did accordingly, with the
utmost dispatch, then they remained about six minutes, with their
firelocks rested and bayonets fixed, but not standing in exact order
I observed a considerable number of young lads, and here and there
a man amongst them, about the middle of the street, facing the soldiers, but not within ten or twelve feet distance from them ; I observed some of them, viz., the lads, &c., had sticks in their hands,
laughing, shouting, huzzaing, and crying fire ; but could not observe
that any of them threw anything at the soldiers, or threatened any
of them. Then the said officer retired from before the soldiers and
stepping behind them, towards the right wing, bid the soldiers
fire ; they not firing, he presently again bid 'em fire, they not
yet firing, he stamped and said, " Damn your bloods, fire, be the
consequence what it will ;" then the second man on the left wing
fired off his gun, then, after a very short pause, they fired one after
another as quick as possible, beginning on the right wing ; the last
man's gun on the left wing flashed in the pan, then he primed again,
and the people being withdrawn from before the soldiers, most of
them further down the street, he turned his gun toward them and
fired upon them. Immediately after the principal firing, I saw
three of the people fall down in the street ; presently after the last
gun was fired off, the said officer, who had commanded the soldiers
(as above) to fire, sprung before them, waving his sword or stick,
said, " Damn ye, rascals, what did ye fire for ?" and struck up the
gun of one of the soldiers who was loading again, whereupon they
seemed confounded and fired no more. I then went up behind them
to the right wing, where one of the people was lying, to see whether
he was dead, where there were four or five people about him, one
of them saying he was dead ; whereupon one of the soldiers said,
" Damn his blood, he is dead, if he ever sprawl again I will be

damned for him." And I remember as the said officer was going down with the soldiers towards the Custom-house, a gentleman spoke to him and said, " Capt. Preston, for God's sake keep your men in order, and mind what you are about." And further I say not.

March 7, 1770. WILLIAM WYAT.

Suffolk, ss. Boston, March 13, 1770. William Wyat, above-named, after due examination, made oath to the truth of the above-written affidavit, taken to perpetuate the re-membrance of the thing.

Before, RI. DANA, Justice of Peace and of the Quorum,
JOHN TUDOR, Justice Peace.

(No. 55.)

I, Henry Knox, of lawful age, testify and say, that between nine and ten o'clock, P. M., the fifth instant, I saw the sentry at the Custom-house charging his musket, and a number of young persons crossing from Royal Exchange to Quaker lane ; seeing him load, stopped and asked him what he meant ? and told others the sentry was going to fire. They then huzzaed and gathered round him at about ten feet distant. I then advancing, went up to him, and the sentry snapped his piece upon them, Knox told him if he fired he died. The sentry answered he did not care, or words to that pur-pose, damning them and saying, if they touched him, he would fire. The boys told him to fire and be damned. Immediately on this I returned to the rest of the people and endeavored to keep every boy from going up, but finding it ineffectual, went off through the crowd and saw a detachment of about eight or nine men and a corporal, headed by Capt. Preston. I took Capt. Preston by the coat and told him for God's sake to take his men back again, for if they fired his life must answer for the consequence ; he replied he was sensible of it, or knew what he was about, or words to that purpose ; and seemed in great haste and much agitated. While I was talking with Capt. Preston, the soldiers of his detachment had attacked the people with their bayonets. There was not the least provocation given to Capt. Preston or his party, the backs of the people being towards them when they were attacked. During the time of the attack I frequently heard the words, " Damn your blood," and such like expressions. When Capt. Preston saw his party engaged he directly left me and went into the crowd, and I departed : the deponent further says that there was not present in King street above seventy or eighty people at the extent, according to his opinion. HENRY KNOX.

Suffolk, ss. Boston, March 17, 1770. Henry Knox, above-named, after due examination, made oath to the truth of the above-written affidavit, taken to perpetuate the re-membrance of the thing.

Before, RI. DANA, Justice of Peace and of the Quorum,
JOHN HILL, Justice Peace.

## (No. 56.)

Edward Payne, of Boston, merchant, testifies and says, that on the evening of the fifth instant, on hearing the bells ring, he supposed there was fire, but on going out he was informed there was not any fire, but a riot of the soldiers, and that the soldiers were cutting down Liberty-tree. That he went into King-street, where he met Mr. Walker the shipwright, who informed him, that the soldiers at Smith's barracks had sallied out upon the inhabitants, and had cut and beat a number of persons, but were drove back to their barracks. That he (the deponent), then went to the east end of the Town House, where he heard the same report from divers persons. That whilst he stood there, a number of persons, not exceeding twenty, some of them with sticks in their hands, came up the lane by Silsby's into King street, at which time there was, as near as he can judge, about the same number in King street, when a lad came up from the Custom-house, and informed the people, that the sentinel there had knocked down a lad belonging to their shop, upon which the people moved that way, and surrounded the sentinel. That this deponent then went home, and stood upon the sill of his entry door, which is nearly opposite to the east end of the Custom-house, where he was soon joined by Mr. George Bethune, and Mr. Harrison Gray, that the people round the sentinel were then crying out " Fire, fire, damn you, why don't you fire," soon after, he perceived a number of soldiers coming down towards the sentinel, with their arms in a horizontal posture, and their bayonets fixed, who turned the people from before the Custom-house, and drew up before the door, the people, who still remained in the street and about the soldiers, continued calling out to them to fire. In this situation they remained some minutes, when he heard a gun snap, and presently a single gun fired and soon after several others went off, one after another, to the number of three or four, and then heard the rammers go into the guns as though they were loading; immediately after which, three or four more went off in the same manner ; at which time, a ball passed through the deponents right arm, upon which he immediately retired into the house. That at the time of the sentinels being surrounded, and at the time of the firing, it appeared to the deponent, that there were from fifty to an hundred persons in the street, and not more. The deponent further saith not.                                                    EDWARD PAYNE.

*Test.* Mr. Payne subscribed his
    name with his left hand.
            JOHN AMÓRY.

Suffolk, ss. Boston, March 21, 1770. Edward Payne, above-named, after due examination, made oath to the truth of the aforesaid affidavit, taken to perpetuate the remembrance of the thing.

Before, JOHN RUDDOCK, Just. Peace and of the Quorum,
    JOHN HILL, Just. Peace.

(No. 57.)

John Gammell, of lawful age, testifies and says, that soon after the bells rang on Monday evening the 5th instant, he stood by the Town House, and saw a party consisting of about fifteen or sixteen soldiers, come out of the main guard, and a serjeant or corporal ordered them to prime and load, which they did ; and a detachment of about six men with a corporal, filed off to William's court, as was said to call Captain Preston, and the rest, to the Custom-house. A few minutes after they took their post by the Custom-house, the deponent went down and saw them pushing at the people with their bayonets, and telling them to stand off, or they would fire upon them ; the people laughed at them ; and told them they dared not to fire. Not long after, the deponent heard the word " Fire," and quickly the man on the right wing fired, and successively several more. On this the deponent walked off through Quaker lane. And further saith not. JOHN GAMMELL.

Suffolk, ss. Boston, March 17, 1770. John Gammell, above-named, after due examination, made oath to the truth of the above affidavit, taken to perpetuate the remembrance of the thing.

Before RI. DANA, Just. of Peace and of the Quorum,
JOHN HILL, Just. of Peace.

(No. 58.)

I, Charlotte Bourgate, of lawful age, an indented servant to Edward Manwaring, Esq. ; being at my master's lodgings at Mr. Hudson's at the north end, on the night of the horrid massacre in King-street, of the 5th instant, heard the bells ring, which I took to be for fire (about half an hour before the bells rung, my master, with one Mr. Munroe, said they would go to the Custom-house and drink a glass of wine) ; then I went out, there being nobody in the house that I knew of, but Mr. Hudson and wife ; then I went up to the Custom-house door and knocked, when a young man, which I have since heard was named Hammond Green, let me in, and locked the door ; when I saw my master and Mr. Munroe come down stairs, and go into a room ; when four or five men went up stairs, pulling and hauling me after them, and said, " My good boy, come ;" when I was carried into the chamber, there was but one light in the room, and that in the corner of the chamber, when I saw a tall man loading a gun (then I saw two guns in the room), my master not being in the chamber, there was a number of gentlemen in the room. After the gun was loaded, the tall man gave it to me, and told me to fire, and said he would kill me if I did not ; I told him I would not. He drawing a sword out of his cane, told me, if I did not fire it, he would run it through my guts. The man putting the gun out of the window, it being a little open, I fired it side way up the street ; the tall man then loaded the gun again. I heard the balls go down. The man then laid it on the window again, and told me to fire it. I told him I would not fire again ; he told me again, he would run me through the guts if I did not. Upon which I fired the same way up the street. After I fired the second gun, I saw my master in the room ; he took a gun and pointed it out of the window ; I heard the gun go off. Then a tall man came and clapped me on the shoulders above and below stairs, and said, that's my good boy, I'll give you some money to morrow. I said, I don't want any money. There being a light in the lower room, and the door being upon the jarr, I saw it was the tall man that clapped me on the shoulder ; then the young man Hammond Green let me out of the door, there being two or three people in the entry ; when I got out of the house, I saw a number of people in the streets. And I ran home as fast as I could, and sat up all night in my master's kitchen. And further say, that my master licked me the next night for telling Mrs. Waldron about his firing out of the Custom-house. And for fear that I should be licked again, I did deny all that I said before Justice Quincy, which I am very sorry for. And further I say not.

    *Attest.* Elisha Story,                his
         Edward Crafts.         CHARLOTTE X BOURGATE,
                                        Mark.

    Suffolk, ss.    Boston, March 23, 1770.    Charlotte Bourgate, above-named, after due examination, made oath to the truth of the above affidavit, Edward Manwaring, Esq., and John Munroe above named, were notified and present ; and interrogated the deponent.    Taken to perpetuate the remembrance of the thing.

    Before, JOHN RUDDOCK, Just. Peace and of the Quorum,
    And, JOHN HILL, Just. Peace.

-----

### (No. 59.)

    Gillam Bass, of lawful age, testifies and says, that being in King street, on Monday night, the 5th instant, after nine of the clock, he saw about an hundred people gathered about the Custom-house, and presently came a party of armed soldiers, with bayonets fixed from the main guard keeping on the south side of King street, till they came nearly opposite the Custom-house, and then passed over, driving through the people in so rough a manner, that it appeared to the deponent that they intended to create a disturbance. They posted themselves between the Custom-house door and the west corner of it ; and in a few minutes began to fire upon the people. Two or three of the flashes so high above the rest, that the deponent verily believes they must have come from the Custom-house windows : And further saith, that he observed no violence to the soldiers at or before the firing, or to the Custom-house, by the people.

                                        GILLAM BASS.

    Suffolk, ss.  Boston, March 16, 1770.  Gillam Bass, above-named, after due examination, made oath to the truth of the above affidavit. Taken to perpetuate the remembrance of the thing.

Before, Ri. DANA, Justice of Peace, and of the Quorum,
JOHN HILL, Justice Peace.

(No. 60.)

Benjamin Alline, of lawful age, testifies and says, that on Monday evening, the 5th current, hearing the bells ring after nine o'clock, he came into King street, and saw the Custom-house sentry standing quietly in his place. About four or five minutes after, the boys in the street came up near to him, and made a noise, on which the soldier returned to the Custom-house steps. The deponent quickly after this saw the Custom-house door open, and the sentry turn that way, and soon shut again. The sentry then faced the boys and waved his gun about as if to keep them off, and in a few minutes eight or nine soldiers came down with an officer at their head, and placed themselves round the sentry, and in a few minutes after, he heard the word Fire, and they fired in succession, one after the other. The deponent further saith, that when he first arrived at the Custom-house, there did not seem to be more than 30 or 40 people round it, mostly boys, and they offered no violence as he observed, only making a noise and huzzaing. And further saith not.
BENJAMIN ALLINE.

Suffolk, ss. Boston, March 17, 1770. Benjamin Alline, above-named, after due examination, made oath to the truth of the above-written affidavit, taken to perpetuate the remembrance of the thing.

Before, Ri. DANA, Just. Peace and of the Quorum,
JOHN HILL, Just. Peace.

(No. 61.)

I, Francis Read, of lawful age, testify, that on Monday evening, the 5th instant, hearing the bells ringing in the centre of the town, I came into King street and found near an hundred people, mostly boys, standing round at about seven or eight yards distance from the Custom-house, before which stood a soldier on sentry. In a few minutes I saw a little man, in a grey surtout with his hair clubbed, open the Custom-house door and go in, and quickly after the sentry went to said door, then a little open, and seemed to speak with somebody in the house, after which the door was shut, and the sentry loaded his piece. In about three or four minutes I saw a party of soldiers come down from the main guard with an officer, which were posted in a semicircle from the door round the sentry-box to the southwest corner of the Custom-house. About five or six minutes after they were posted, I heard the word "Fire," from among the soldiers, and in a little time after the soldiers fired; first one gun, then another, some times two at once, till eight or ten were fired. Casting my eyes about after the firing was over, I saw the smoke of two discharges high above the rest. On this I left the place, and further say not.
FRANCIS READ.

Suffolk, ss.   Boston, March 20, 1770.   Francis Read, above-
    named, after due examination, made oath to the truth of
    the aforesaid affidavit, taken to perpetuate the remem-
    brance of the thing.
Before, JOHN RUDDOCK, Just. Peace and of the Quorum,
    And, BELCHER NOYES, Just. Peace.

---

(No. 62.)

I, Dimond Morton, of lawful age, testify and say, that on Monday
night the 5th instant, between the hours of nine and ten I heard the
cry of fire by my house.   Immediately I ran out towards the Town-
House ; when I got between the Old South Meeting and the Old-
Brick Meeting, I met some people, they told me there was no fire,
but people gathered in King street ; immediately I left them and
came towards the Town-House, when I saw a number of people go
round the Brazen-head corner, some crying, they are this way, and I
run in amongst them, and came down before the Custom-house, and
there I saw a sentinel walking backwards and forwards before the
door.   Soon after I saw the sentinel retreat back upon the stone of
the Custom-house door, waving his bayonet breast high all the way.
When he got on the stone he drew his cartridge to load his gun ; whilst
he was loading his gun, I saw Thomas Greenwood, a waiter to the
commissioners, run out from the people where I was, and run behind
the sentinel, and knock at the door of the Customs, and was soon
let in : By that time the sentinel had his gun loaded.   Then the
people cried, you dare not fire ; and others said, fire and be damned ;
then the boys gave two or three cheers.   Upon that I saw Capt.
Preston, marching and leading down from the main guard eight or
ten soldiers, with their bayonets fixed, swinging their guns.   When
they passed me, I followed them down to the Custom-house.   In
about two minutes, Capt. Preston or some other person ordered
them to load, which they did ; then I went towards Quaker lane,
when I saw the flash of a gun from the soldiers at the Custom-house,
and a man fall before me ; the guns being repeatedly fired, I looked
round and saw two or three men lay down on the snow.   When I
found there were three dead, and a number of others wounded, in about
ten or fifteen minutes afterwards, I saw the soldiers march towards
the main guard—the snow being at that time near a foot deep——
And I further say, that I did not see any insult offered to the sentinel from the inhabitants ; and at the time the guns were fired, there
were not above sixty or seventy persons standing before the Custom-
house door.   And further I say not.                DIMOND MORTON.
Suffolk, ss.   Boston, March 17, 1770.   Dimond Morton, above-
    named, after due examination, made oath to the truth of
    the above-written affidavit, taken to perpetuate the remem-
    brance of the thing.
Before, RI. DANA, Just. of Peace and of the Quorum,
    And, JOHN HILL, Just. Peace.

APPENDIX.

## (No. 63.)

Benjamin Frizel, of Pownalborough, in the County of Lincoln, mariner, of lawful age, testifieth and saith, that in the evening of the 5th day of March current, going to Capt. Joseph Henshaw's at the south part of Boston, in his way thither, under Liberty Tree, exactly at eight o'clock of said evening, he saw there eleven soldiers, and an officer met them, dressed in a blue surtout ; upon his speaking to them, they appeared very submissive, the officer ordering them to appear at their respective places at the time, and if they should see any of the inhabitants of the town, or any other people not belonging to them, with arms, clubs, or any other warlike weapons, more than two being assembled together, to order them to stop, and ask them their business, and where they were going ; if they refused to stop, or tell them their business or separate themselves, to stop them with their firelocks, and all that shall take their part. After giving these orders, the officer went off to the northward, and the soldiers southward ; upon which the deponent proceeded about his business as far as Wheeler's point, and while there, the bell rang as usual for fire, and he with others ran to the Town-house ; two engines being there drawn, the men attending, left them on the west end of the Town-house, and going with others into King street, were stopped by two sentinels of the main guard, and forbid to pass on their peril, and said if they did, they would fire on them ; but one man somewhat bolder than the rest, said as the bells rang for fire, and all the inhabitants of the town had good right to pass through any street or lane of the town, he should pass, and shouldering a stick he had in his hand, went forward and was followed by the deponent and many others into King street, the deponent taking his station at the west corner of the house now called the Custom-house, and between the corner and the sentry-box, where standing about two or three minutes, he saw six or seven soldiers come from the opposite side of the street, near to the head or opening of Royal Exchange lane, where they halted, and some of them spoke to the sentry at the Custom-house and faced about, in which posture they stood about two minutes, and in that time he heard nothing said to them, or of them, by any of the inhabitants; but heard two or three cheers given by the people, and two or three boatswain's calls piped, upon the last of which the soldiers began their fire, the deponent still standing at the corner of the Custom-house, the first discharge being only one gun, the next of two guns, upon which the deponent thinks he saw a man stumble ; the third discharge was of three guns, upon which he thinks he saw two men fall, and immediately after were discharged five guns, two of which were by soldiers on his right hand, the other three, as appeared to the deponent, were discharged from the balcony or the chamber window of the Custom-house, the flashes appearing on the left hand and higher than the right hand flashes appeared to be, and of which the deponent was very sensible, although his eyes were much turned to the soldiers who were all on his right hand ; soon after this, the deponent saw five men on the ground, three whereof appeared to be dead, and the other two to be struggling ; for the space of two minutes following all action ceased ; after which the general cry was, let us pick up the dead, and not let the soldiers have them, and thereupon the deponent assisted in supporting and steadying one who was wounded till a chair was brought to carry him off.

BENJAMIN FRIZEL.

Suffolk, ss.   Boston, March 22, 1770.   Benjamin Frizel, above-mentioned, after due examination, made oath to the truth of the aforesaid affidavit, taken to perpetuate the remembrance of the thing.

Before, JOHN RUDDOCK, Just. Peace and of the Quorum,
JOHN HILL, Just. Peace.

---

### (No. 64.)

Jeremiah Allen, of lawful age, testifies and says, that in the evening of the fifth day of March current, being at about nine o'clock in the front chamber of the house occupied by Col. Ingersol in King street, he heard some guns fired, which occasioned his going into the balcony of the said house—that when he was in the said balcony, in company with Mr. William Molineux, Jr., and John Simpson, he heard the discharge of four or five guns, the flashes of which appeared to be to the westward of the sentry box ; and immediately after, he the deponent heard two or three more guns, and saw the flashes thereof from out of the house now called the Custom-house, as they evidently appeared to him, and which he the said deponent at the same time declared to the aforesaid Molineux and Simpson, being then near him, saying to them, at the same time pointing his hand towards the Custom-house, "there they are out of the Custom-house."   And further the deponent saith not.

JEREMIAH ALLEN.

Suffolk, ss.   The above-named Jeremiah Allen, personally appearing, and being carefully examined, and duly cautioned to testify the whole truth, maketh solemn oath to the forewritten deposition by him subscribed, taken to perpetuate the remembrance of the thing.

Before, RI. DANA, Justice of Peace and of the Quorum,
JOHN HILL, Justice Peace.

---

### (No. 65.)

Josiah Simpson, of lawful age, testifieth and saith, that on the evening of the fifth of March current, at about nine of the clock, he heard a bell ringing at the south part of the town, which caused him to leave his shop to make inquiry.   Soon after, he heard that the soldiers had rose upon the inhabitants ; but when he had got as far as Faneuil Hall, seeing a number of gentlemen standing together. the deponent made up to them, and asked them what the disturbance was ; they answered him that two young men had been abused by the soldiers—but that the soldiers had now returned to their barracks—he then proceeded with a number of others up Royal Exchange lane ; at the head of the lane some of the persons with him cried out, here is a soldier, and huzzaed. Immediately the soldier who was sentry near to the box before the Custom-house, repaired to the Custom-house door, at which with the knocker the soldier gave three very hard strokes—upon which some person within side opened the door and spoke to him remarkably short, and then shut it again. The soldier then directly loaded his gun, knocking the breech twice hard upon the stone steps ; at the same time seven soldiers (as the deponent judges), with a commanding officer, came and cried clear the way, as he came along : then forming them into a half circle, ordered them to load ; the deponent then made up as he could to the officer, and said, for God's sake don't fire upon the people ; he made him no answer ; then turning to the inhabitants, he the deponent expressed himself in the following manner : for God's sake don't trouble these men for they are upon duty and will fire—turning about to the soldiers he saw them making up to the inhabitants, with their bayonets fixed (about ten feet off), directing them to stand off, attempting to drive them away with their bayonets—then he withdrew himself to the other side of the way, where seeing a man attempt to throw a club, he begged that he would not, adding that if he did the soldiers would fire, and he did not. The deponent then standing by Warden and Vernon's shop on the south side of King street, with his back to the soldiers ; immediately after heard the word present, at which word he stooped down. A little space of time ensued, and then he heard the words, " Damn you, fire ;" the sound of which words seemed to proceed from the left of all the soldiers, and very near to the sentry box ; upon this order, he judged two guns were discharged, and immediately three more, and then two more—one of the two last guns went about five or six inches over the deponent's back—after which he stood up, and another gun was discharged which wounded one Robert Patterson in the arm, and the blood was sprinkled upon the deponent's hand and waistcoat. After the firing the deponent saw four persons drop ; then looking towards the soldiers, the deponent saw them making towards the inhabitants with their fixed bayonets ; upon which he retired down Quaker lane, and went round into the main street homewards, where he met a number of people going up Royal Exchange lane—from thence he retired home.

JOSIAH SIMPSON.

The deponent further saith that he is satisfied there was not more than seventy or eighty people in King street, who offered no violence to the soldiers or to any other persons, nor threatened any.

JOSIAH SIMPSON.

Suffolk, ss. Boston, March 16, 1770. Josiah Simpson, above-named, after due examination, made oath to the truth of

6

the afore-written affidavit, taken to perpetuate the remembrance of the thing.

Before, Ri. Dana, Just. Peace and of the Quorum,
John Hill, Just. Peace.

(No. 66.)

I, John Wilson, of lawful age, testify, that on Monday evening the 5th current, I was at Mr. Burdett's at the head of Long-lane, and heard the bells ring and fire cried, and thereupon went in company with others to King street, and saw no disturbance there ; hearing the bells still ringing, I asked what was the matter ? The people said the soldiers had insulted the inhabitants, on which I went to Cornhill, where the bustle had been, and found no soldiers there. Then I came down King street opposite the Custom-house, and saw a man with a light colored surtout coming from the main guard go up to the sentry, and lay his hand on his shoulder and speak some words to the sentry, and then enter the Custom-house door. On this the sentry grounded the breech of his gun, took out a cartridge, primed and loaded, and shouldered his firelock. After this I drew back opposite Mr. Stone's, and in a few minutes saw a party of soldiers headed by an officer coming down from the main guard, crying to the inhabitants, "Damn you, make way you boogers !" I not moving from my place, was struck by one of them on the hip with the butt of his musket, which bruised me so much that it was next day very sore, and much discolored. The officer seeing the soldier strike me, said to the soldier in an angry manner, "Why don't you prick the boogers ?" The party drew up before the Custom-house door, and ranged to the west corner in a half circle, and charged their pieces breast high. Some small boys coming up made a noise to the soldiers, on which the officer said to them, "Why don't you fire ? Damn you, fire !" They hereupon fired, and two men fell dead in my sight. I then left the place, and went over the street and assisted Patterson the wounded man in getting home. The deponent further saith, that when he got into King street he saw nobody but the sentry walking backwards and forwards by the Custom-house, and then went to Cornhill as above ; and at the time of firing he verily believes there were not above fifty persons in the street near the Custom-house, the snow being at that time near a foot deep ; and further I say not.          John Wilson.

Suffolk, ss.   Boston, March 19, 1770.   John Wilson, above-named, after due examination, made oath to the truth of the above-written affidavit, taken to perpetuate the remembrance of the thing.

Before, Ri. Dana, Justice of the Peace and of the Quorum,
And, John Hill, Justice Peace.

(No. 67.)

George Costar, of the Bay of Bulls, in the island of Newfoundland, mariner, of lawful age, testifieth and saith, that being in Boston, about nine of the clock, in the evening of the 5th day of March current, he, the deponent was standing in King street, near the middle of said street, and while there standing, among a large number of other people, in about five or six minutes after he stopped, he heard the word of command given to the soldiers, " Fire," upon which one gun was fired, which did no execution, as the deponent observed. About half a minute after, two guns, one of which killed one Samuel Gray, a ropemaker, the other, a mulatto man, between which two men the deponent stood ; after this the deponent heard the discharge of four or five guns more, by the soldiers ; immediately after which the deponent heard the discharge of two guns or pistols from an open window of the middle story of the Custom-house, near to the place where the sentry box was placed, and being but a small distance from the window, he heard the people from within speak and laugh, and soon after he saw the casement lowered down ; after which the deponent assisted others in carrying off one of the corpses.

his

GEORGE V. ꓶ COSTER,

mark.

Suffolk, ss.  Boston, March 16, 1770.  George Coster, above-
named, after due examination, made oath to the truth of
the above-written affidavit, taken to perpetuate the remembrance of the thing.

Before, RI. DANA, Just. of Peace and of the Quorum,
And, JOHN HILL, Just. Peace.

(No. 68.)

Samuel Drowne, of Boston, of lawful age, testifieth and saith, that about nine of the clock of the evening of the fifth day of March current, standing at his own door in Cornhill, saw about fourteen or fifteen soldiers of the 29th regiment, who came from Murray's barrack, some of whom were armed with naked cutlasses, swords, or bayonets, others with clubs, fire shovels, or tongs, and came upon the inhabitants of the town, then standing or walking in Cornhill, and abused some and violently assaulted others as they met them, most of whom were without so much as a stick in their hands to defend themselves, as the deponent very clearly could discern, it being moon-light, and himself being one of the assaulted persons.  All or most of the said soldiers he saw go by the way of Cornhill, Crooked lane, and Royal Exchange lane into King street, and there followed them, and soon discovered them to be quarrelling and fighting with the people whom they saw there, which the deponent thinks were not more than a dozen, when the soldiers came there first, armed as aforesaid.  Of those dozen people, the most of them were gentlemen, standing together a little below the town-house upon the Exchange.  At the appearance of those soldiers so armed, the most of the twelve persons went off, some of them being first assaulted. After which the said soldiers were observed by the deponent to go towards the main-guard, from whence were at the same time issuing and coming into King street, five soldiers of said guard and a corporal armed with firelocks, who called out to the fore-mentioned soldiers armed with cutlasses, &c., and said to them, " Go away," on which they dispersed and went out of King street, some one way and some another—by this time were collected together in King street about two hundred people, and then the deponent stood upon the steps of the Exchange tavern, being the next house to the Custom-house ; and soon after saw Capt. Preston, whom he well knew, with a number of soldiers armed with firelocks, drawn up near the west corner of the Custom-house ; and at that instant the deponent thinks so great a part of the people were dispersed at the sight of the armed soldiers, as that not more than twenty or thirty remained in King street ;[*] those who did remain being mostly sailors and other persons meanly dressed, called out to the armed soldiers and dared them to fire, upon which the deponent heard Capt. Preston say to the soldiers, " Damn your bloods ! why don't you fire ?" The soldiers not regarding those words of their captain, he immediately said, " Fire." Upon which they fired irregularly, pointing their guns variously in a part of a circle as they stood : during the time of the soldiers firing, the deponent saw the flashes of two guns fired from the Custom-house, one of which was out of a window of the chamber westward of the balcony, and the other from the balcony, the gun which he clearly discerned being pointed through the ballisters, and the person who held the gun in a stooping posture, withdraw himself into the house, having a handkerchief or some kind of cloth over his face. After this the deponent assisted in carrying off the dead and wounded, as soon as the soldiers would permit the people so to do, for at first they were cruel enough to obstruct the carrying them off.                          SAMUEL DROWNE.

Suffolk, ss.   Boston, March 16, 1770.   The above-named Samuel Drowne personally appearing, and being carefully examined and duly cautioned to testify the whole truth, maketh solemn oath to the fore-written deposition by him subscribed, taken to perpetuate the remembrance of the thing.

Before, RI. DANA, Just. of Peace and of the Quorum,
    And, JOHN HILL, Just. of Peace.

---

[*] Mr. Drowne says there were collected together in King street about two hundred persons, and that at the sight of the armed soldiers, they so far dispersed, as that not more than twenty or thirty remained in King street.

This circumstance accounts for the diversity in some of the depositions, with regard to the number of persons in King street about that time : such depositions probably referring to different moments—*moments*, because the whole disturbance in King street, from its beginning to the firing, continued but a short space of time.

## (No. 69.)

I, Robert Patterson, of lawful age, testify and say, that on Monday night, the 5th current, being at Capt. McNeill's at the North End, heard the bells ring and " Fire!" cried. I immediately ran till I got into Royal Exchange lane, it being about a quarter after 9 o'clock. I saw a number of people in the lane. I asked what was the matter? They told me that the soldiers were going to kill all the inhabitants. I immediately went through the lane, and stood in the middle of King street about ten or eleven minutes (the sentinel then standing leaning against his box), when I saw an officer with seven or eight soldiers coming from the main-guard, clearing the way with their guns and bayonets, go below the sentinel box, and turn up and place themselves around it, facing the people standing opposite Royal Exchange lane ; when I saw a man with a light colored surtout at the Custom-house door, the door being wide open, there standing with his shoulder against the side ; then I heard the officer order the soldiers to load, which they did. After that I heard the people say, " Damn you, why don't you fire ?" In about a minute after I heard the word " Fire !" (but from whom I cannot say) which the soldiers did. Looking round I saw three men lay dead on the snow; the snow being at that time near a foot deep. Immediately they loaded again. The people then gave three cheers, and cried out, " Let's go in upon them, and prevent their firing again;" upon which they put on their hats and advanced towards them. My hand being raised to put on my hat, still advancing towards the soldiers, the sentinel up with his gun and fired, the balls going through my lower right arm, my hand immediately falling; and finding myself wounded, made the best of my way home with help. And further I say not.

Attest. Elisha Story.    ROBERT + PATTERSON,
mark. his

Suffolk, ss. Boston, March 20, 1770. Robert Patterson, above-named, after due examination, made oath to the truth of the aforesaid affidavit, taken to perpetuate the remembrance of the thing.

Before, JOHN RUDDOCK, Just. Peace and of the **Quorum,**
And, JOHN HILL, Just. Peace.

## (No. 70.)

Cato, a negro man, servant to Tuthil Hubbart, Esq., being of lawful age, testifies and says, that on Monday evening, the fifth of March current, on his hearing the cry of " Fire !" he ran into King street, where he saw a number of people assembled before the Custom-house ; that he stood near the sentry box and saw the soldiers fire on the people, who stood in the middle of said street ; directly after which he saw two flashes of guns, one quick upon the other, from the chamber-window of the Custom-house ; and that after the firing was all over, while the people were carrying away the dead

and wounded, he saw the Custom-house door opened, and several soldiers (one of whom had a cutlass) go into the Custom-house and shut the door after them ; that before the soldiers fired he heard a voice saying, " Damn you, why don't you fire ?" but did not see who it was.                                                        his
   Test. John Edwards.                              CATO ( c.
                                                    mark.

    Suffolk, ss.  Boston, March 16, 1770.  The above-named Cato, after careful examination, made oath to the truth of the above-written affidavit, taken to perpetuate the remembrance of the thing.
      Before, RI. DANA, Just. of Peace and of the Quorum,
      And, JOHN HILL, Just. of Peace.

                        (No. 71.)

    Daniel Usher, of lawful age, testifies and says, that coming into King street about half after nine o'clock on Monday evening the 5th current, he saw several persons, mostly young folks, gathered between the Town House and Coffee House, some of whom were talking to the sentinel at the Commissioners' or Custom-house ; after some time, the boys at a distance began to throw light snow-balls at him, which he seemed much enraged at, and went on to the Custom-house steps, where he appeared to have charged his gun, giving it a heavy stamp upon the door step, as if to force down the lead ; and then swore to the boys if they came near him he would blow their brains out.  About ten minutes after this, the deponent saw Capt. Preston leading seven or eight men from towards the Town House, and placed them between the Custom-house door, and the sentinel box.  About four or five minutes after they were posted, the snow-balls now and then coming towards the soldiers, the Capt. commanded them to fire.  Upon this, one gun quickly went off ; and afterwards he said " Fire by all means !" others succeeding, and the deponent being utterly unarmed, to avoid further danger, went up round the Town House till the fray was over.  And further saith not.                                              DANIEL USHER.
    Suffolk, ss.  March 16, 1770.  The above-named Daniel Usher, personally appearing, and being carefully examined, and duly cautioned to testify the whole truth, maketh solemn oath to the fore-written deposition, by him subscribed, taken to perpetuate the remembrance of the thing.
      Before, RI. DANA, Justice of the Peace and of the Quorum,
      And, JOHN HILL, Just. Peace.

                        (No. 72.)

    I, Robert Goddard, of lawful age, testify and declare, that on Monday evening, the 5th instant, between the hours of 9 and 10 o'clock, being at my house at Wheeler's point, I heard the cry of fire.  I ran out, and came through Long lane into King street, right up to the north-west side of the Town House; when I got there, I saw a number of gentleman, standing and talking, and heard them say, that there was a man stabbed through the arm, and that it was very hard that the people could not pass the streets without being stabbed. Immediately after, I heard some people cry out for assistance. I then went down into King street, and in going down, overtook an officer (as I thought), with eight or nine soldiers, with bayonets charged breast high, the officer holding a naked cutlass in his hand, swinging, and calling stand out of the way, and the soldiers cursing and damning, and pushing their bayonets, to clear the way. They went down to the Custom-house, and placed themselves just above the sentinel box; the officer then ordered the soldiers to place themselves, which they did, in a half circle; with that the boys came up near to the soldiers (standing as before). The officer then said, boys go off, lest there be some murder done; with that the boys removed back a little distance, throwing snow-balls, the soldiers pushing them with their bayonets, saying, damn you, stand off; with that the boys went forward again, and a man with a naked cutlass in his hand, who appeared to be the commanding officer (as before), gave the word fire; immediately a gun going off upon the left of me, I saw a man like a sailor, go up to the commander, and strike him upon the left arm. Immediately he, the said officer, said "Think I'll be used in this manner, damn you, fire," which they did, one after another. After they had all fired, he ordered them to prime and load again; after that he ordered his men in the middle of the street, and told them to clear their way, with their bayonets breast high; with that, looking round, I saw four men lay dead on the snow, the snow being at that time near a foot deep. Then I went and helped the mulatto man who was shot into Mr. Stone's house. After we got him in there, I saw him give one gasp. I then opened his breast, and saw two holes, one in each breast, where the balls had entered. After that went to the door, and looked, and saw the soldiers standing in the middle of the street, and saw two gentlemen talking with the officers and soldiers. Presently after, went to see the mulatto again; and returned back into the street, saw all the soldiers at the main guard-house out, with their bayonets charged breast high; with that going home through Quaker-lane into Long-lane, about the middle of the lane, saw two soldiers, who told me to stand out of the way, or else they would stab me. I immediately got out of the way, and made the best of my way home. And further say, that the grand jury desired me to go and see whether I should know the officer again; one of them going with me, I went up, and when I came to the jail, I saw several people in the room with him. The gentleman of the grand jury (who went up with me), asked me which was the man, I told him that that gentleman (pointing to Capt. Preston), looked very much like the man, and I verily believed he was the man that ordered the soldiers to fire. "Don't you say so," says he; "Yes, sir," said I, "you look very much like the man." "If you say so," said he, clapping his hands, " I am ruined, and undone." And further say, that at the time of firing, there was but about fifty or sixty persons, mostly boys, in King street.                    ROBERT GODDARD.

 Suffolk, ss. Boston, March 22, 1770. Robert Goddard, afore-named, after due examination, made oath to the truth of the aforesaid affidavit, taken to perpetuate the remembrance of the thing.

Before, JOHN RUDDOCK, Just. Peace and of the Quorum, And, JOHN HILL, Just. Peace.

----

(No. 73.)

I, John Hickling, being of lawful age, testify and say, that on Monday the 5th day of March 1770, returning from New Boston in the evening between the hours of nine and ten o'clock, I heard a noise and the cry of fire in King street, and inquiring the cause was informed the soldiers intended to fire on the inhabitants ; immediately proceeding to the place, I saw eight or nine soldiers with fixed bayonets, charged breast high, standing in a circular manner at the corner of the Custom-house, and an officer standing before them at the end of the bayonets, between the soldiers and the inhabitants. I saw but a few scattering people, supposed to be about thirty, in the street before them at that time, and therefore was at a loss for the reason of such an appearance ; going up to the officer I found a young man named Bliss talking with him ; I inquired his name of Bliss, who informed me that it was Preston. At that instant Mr. Richard Palmes came up and asked the officer if he intended to fire upon the people ? He answered, " By no means." Palmes asked if the guns were loaded ? Preston. answered in the affirmative. Palmes further asked, " With powder and ball ?" Preston answered they were. The soldiers, during this conversation, assumed different postures, shoving their bayonets frequently at the people, one in particular pushing against my side swore he would run me through ; I laid hold of his bayonet and told him that nobody was going to meddle with them. Not more than ten seconds after this I saw something white, resembling a piece of snow or ice, fall among the soldiers, which knocked the end of a firelock to the ground. At that instant the word " Fire !" was given, but by whom I know not ; but concluded it did not come from the officer aforesaid, as I was within a yard of him and must have heard him had he spoken it, but am satisfied said Preston did not forbid them to fire ; I instantly leaped within the soldier's bayonet as I heard him cock his gun, which that moment went off between Mr. Palmes and myself. I, thinking there was nothing but powder fired, stood still, till upon the other side of Mr. Palmes and close to him, I saw another gun fired, and the man since called Attucks, fall. I then withdrew about two or three yards, and turning, saw Mr. Palmes upon his knee, and the soldiers pushing at him with their bayonets. During this the rest of the guns were fired, one after another, when I saw two more fall. I ran to one and seeing the blood gush out of his head though just expiring, I felt for the wound and found a hole as big as my hand. This I have since learned was Mr. Gray. I then went to Attucks and found him gasping, pulled his head out of the gutter and left him ; I returned to the soldiers and asked them what they thought of themselves, and whether they did not deserve to be cut to pieces, to lay men wallowing in their blood in such a manner ? They answered, " God damn them, they should have stood out of our way." The soldiers were then loading their muskets, and told me upon my peril not to come any nearer to them. I further declare that I heard no other affront given them than the huzzaing and whistling of boys in the street. JOHN HICKLING.

Suffolk, ss. Boston, March 16, 1770. The above-named John Hickling, personally appearing, and being carefully examined and duly cautioned to testify the whole truth, maketh solemn oath to the fore-written deposition by him subscribed, taken to perpetuate the remembrance of the thing.
Before, RI. DANA, Just. of Peace and of the Quorum,
And, JOHN HILL, Just. Peace.

---

(No. 74.)

I, Obadiah Whiston, of lawful age, testify and say, that on the evening of the 5th instant, being at a house in Pond lane, on hearing the bells ring, ran towards King street, and in going I met a person who said, there is no fire, but the soldiers are fighting with the inhabitants. I went down the north side of the Town-House into King street, and there was only a few scattering people in said street ; I came up to the Brazenhead in Cornhill, and saw a barber's boy, who told me he had been struck by the soldiers ; then I went to the south side of the Town-House and stood near the main-guard, where a considerable number of persons stood. Captain Preston standing by the guard-house door, said, " Damn you, turn out, guard," which they obeyed, and then took off seven or eight soldiers from the right, and went down King street, where I with the chief of the people followed, and in going down the soldiers pushed me and said, stand out of the way ; I followed them (to see where they were going) as far as the Custom-house, where said Preston drew them up, and some boys being in the street, huzzaed ; a few minutes after as I stood there, I saw one gun go off, and several more were fired directly after ; the people near me said there was some persons killed, after which I saw one man dead.

OBADIAH WHISTON

Suffolk, ss. Boston, March 21, 1770. Obadiah Whiston, abovenamed, after due examination, made oath to the truth of the above affidavit, taken to perpetuate the remembrance of the thing.
Before, JOHN RUDDOCK, Just. Peace and of the Quorum,
JOHN HILL, Just. Peace.

(No. 75.)

George Robert Twelves Hewes, of lawful age, testifies and says, that on the last night, about one o'clock, as he was returning alone from his house to the Town-House, he met Sergeant Chambers of the 29th, with eight or nine soldiers, all with very large clubs and cutlasses, when Dobson, a soldier, spoke to him and asked him how he fared, he told him very badly, to see his townsmen shot in such a manner, and asked him if he did not think it was a dreadful thing ; said Dobson swore by God it was a fine thing, and said you shall see more of it ; and on perceiving I had a cane, he informed Sergeant Chambers of it, who seized and forced it from me, saying I had no right to carry it ; I told him I had as good a right to carry a cane as they had to carry clubs, but they hurried off with it into the main guard. GEORGE ROBERT TWELVES HEWES.

March 6, 1770. The deponent further adds, that just before the soldiers came from the main guard·to the Custom-house, there were about fifteen or sixteen little boys near the sentry, who was standing on the steps of the Custom-house ;. and he saw a young man of a middling stature, with a grey coat and short curled hair, press by the sentinel towards the door of the Custom-house and knock at said door, upon which some person came and opened the door and he went in and shut the door immediately after him ; and at the same time the snow was near a foot deep in King street.

GEORGE ROBERT TWELVES HEWES.

Suffolk, ss. Boston, March 17, 1770. George Robert Twelves Hewes, above-named, after due examination, made oath to the truth of the aforesaid affidavit, taken to perpetuate the remembrance of the thing.

Before, RI. DANA, Just. of Peace and of the Quorum,
JOHN HILL, Just. of Peace.

---

(No. 76.)

I, Thomas Jackson, Jr., do testify and declare, that on Monday, the fifth instant in the evening, being in company, I heard (as near as I can recollect), between nine and ten o'clock, a drum beat to arms ; 1 immediately told the gentlemen (with whom I was then engaged), I imagined there was some disturbance between the inhabitants and the soldiery ; he replied, foh ! I believe it is nothing but boys. I told him I was afraid there was something more in it than that, and desired him (as the drum approached us), to look out of the window to see whether they were soldiers or not. He immediately opened the window, and told me they were soldiers. Upon this information, I immediately put on my hat and went out. I had not gone many paces before I met a man, of whom I inquired the reason of the drum beating. He told me there were six men killed in King street by the military ; I immediately hastened on in my way to King street, and met another person by Concert hall, of whom I likewise inquired as aforesaid ; his answer to me corresponded with the other. When I got into King street, I found a great number of people there assembled, and intended going into the Custom-house, to find out the particulars of the affair. Upon my knocking at the Custom-house door with the knocker, Mr. Hammond Green (who was then looking out of the window), asked me, " Who was there ?" I called him by name, and told him I wanted to come into the Custom-house. He told me he would not let me, nor even his father, (and I think he said,) nor one of the Commissioners, into the house, for he had orders for so doing, or to that effect. I immediately quitted the door and stayed some time at the bottom, and then at the head of the Town-house, where I met Capt. John Riordan. While we were conversing, a party of the 29th regiment came down Queen street, and joined the regiment then at the Town-house ; soon after that, I asked Capt. Riordan if he would spend an hour at the coffee-house ; he complied, and we immediately went ; after spending some time there, I went home, and in going home ; I found the inhabitants were gone off and the soldiers gone from the Town-house. It was some time before I came into King street, that the guns were fired, and when I knocked at the Custom-house door, all the persons I saw at the window over the sentry-box at the Custom-house (which window was then opened), was Mr. Hammond Green, and some women. THO. JACKSON, JR.

Suffolk, ss. Boston, March 16, 1770. Thomas Jackson, Jun., above-named, after due examination, made oath to the truth of the above-written affidavit, taken to perpetuate the remembrance of the thing.

Before, RI. DANA, Just. of Peace and of the Quorum,
JOHN HILL, Just. of Peace.

(No. 77.)

I, John Riordan, of lawful age, testify, that on Monday evening the fifth instant, between 10 and 11 o'clock, I was at the British coffee-house and heard Mr. Wells, the master of the Rose man-of-war, say that he had done more than ever he did in his life, pointing to his hat, out of which he had pulled the cockade, and continued, that all the boats were hoisted out, the barge particularly, which had not been before for four months. Said master had at the same time something that appeared like arms under his coat, which he said were good stuff—that he knew of this before (meaning as I thought the massacre of that evening) and had sent one boat after another on shore for orders, but having no return, had come himself in the barge. JOHN RIORDAN.

Suffolk, ss. Boston, March 20, 1770. John Riordan, above-named, after due examination, made oath to the truth of the aforesaid affidavit, taken to perpetuate the remembrance of the thing.

Before, JOHN RUDDOCK, Just. Peace and of the Quorum,
JOHN HILL, Just. of Peace.

(No. 78.)

Abraham Tuckerman, of lawful age, testifies and says, that James Vibart, quarter-master of the 29th regiment, about ten o'clock A.M., the 8th instant, said, the troubles here were nothing to what they would be in six months.   Being asked why he thought so, replied, This affair will get home, and the people here will be disarmed as they are in Ireland.                         ABRAHAM TUCKERMAN.

Suffolk, ss. Boston, March 16, 1770.   Abraham Tuckerman, above-named, after due examination, made oath to the truth of the afore-written affidavit, taken to perpetuate the remembrance of the thing.

Before, RI. DANA, Just. Peace and of the Quorum,
JOHN HILL, Just. Peace.

---

(No. 79.)

Spencer Walker, of Boston, tailor, of lawful age, testifies and says, that on the evening of the 5th instant, (being a bright moon-light evening) immediately after the massacre in King street, he was passing alone, by Murray's barrack, and was attacked by a man of middle height and pretty lusty, a rough countenance and hair curled round his head, whom he took to be an officer in disguise ; that the said officer rushed out of the gate from behind two soldiers with a drawn sword in his hand, and seized the deponent first by the collar and asked him why he carried a stick, to which the deponent answered it was all he had to defend himself with ; the officer then seized his stick and swore he would take it from him ; the depo-nent said he should not ; the officer then pulled the stick three times and drew back his sword as though he would make a pass at him, upon which the deponent let go the stick and turned back and saw at the front door of the house another officer talking with a woman ; the deponent asked the officer if he kept soldiers there to disarm people as they went about their proper business, upon which the officer laughed at him ; the deponent then told the officer that he would think it very hard if any inhabitant had taken a gun from a soldier as he was going to relieve a sentry, the officer again laughed at him ; upon which a soldier came up and struck the deponent on the hip with the breech end of his gun in the presence of the officer at the door, and then the deponent retired.   The deponent further says, that the next day he saw the same person who took the stick from him (knowing him to be the same) in the dress of a commission-officer of the 29th regiment.                  SPENCER WALKER.

Suffolk, ss. Boston, March 20, 1770.   Spencer Walker, above-named, after due examination, made oath to the truth of the above-written affidavit, taken to perpetuate the re-membrance of the thing.

Before, JOHN RUDDOCK, Justice of Peace and of the Quorum,
JOHN HILL, Justice Peace.

(No. 80.)

Jonathan Mason, of lawful age, testifies and says, that on the evening of the 5th of March 1770, about 10 o'clock, being in King street, Boston, standing near his Honor the Lieut. Governor, he heard him say to an officer at the head of the King's troops, who it was said was Captain Preston, Sir, you are sensible you had no right to fire, unless you had orders from a magistrate. To which Capt. Preston replied, Sir, we were insulted, or words to that purpose, upon which Capt. Preston desired his Honor to go with him to the guard-house, which his Honor declined, and repaired to the council chamber. JONA. MASON.

Suffolk, ss. Boston, March 21, 1770. Jonathan Mason, above-named, after due examination, made oath to the truth of the aforesaid affidavit, taken to perpetuate the remembrance of the thing.

Before, JOHN RUDDOCK, Just. Peace and of the Quorum,
JOHN HILL, Just. Peace.

---

(No. 81.)

I, Isaac Pierce, of Boston, of lawful age, testify and say, that on Monday evening, the 5th instant, hearing the bells ring, and that the main guard had fired on the inhabitants, repaired to King street, and found the 29th regiment drawn up between the State-house and main guard-house, and facing down said street, towards the inhabitants; and seeing his Honor the Commander-in-Chief appear, I went with him towards the soldiers, the front rank having their fire-locks presented, with bayonets fixed; when we came near, I spoke to Capt. Preston, then on the right, telling him there was his Honor the Commander-in-Chief; Capt. Preston said "Where," I said (pointing to his Honor), "*There*, and you are presenting your fire-locks at him," on which his Honor went round on the right flank, and coming to Capt. Preston, said "Sir, are you the commanding officer," who answered, "Yes, sir;" his Honor then said, "Do you know, sir, you have no power to fire on any body of people collected together, except you have a civil magistrate with you, to give orders;" Capt. Preston answered, "I was obliged to, to save my sentry," on which I immediately said, "Then you have murdered three or four men to save your sentry." ISAAC PIERCE.

Suffolk, ss. Boston, March 21, 1770. Isaac Pierce, above-named, after due examination, made oath to the truth of the aforesaid affidavit, taken to perpetuate the remembrance of the thing.

Before, JOHN RUDDOCK, Just. Peace and of the Quorum,
JOHN HILL, Just. Peace.

---

(No. 82.)

I, Ebenezer Dorr, of lawful age, testify and say, that on the evening of the 5th instant, hearing the bells ring in the centre of the town, I came down to the Town-house and saw the 29th regiment under arms, between the Town-house and main-guard, their lines extending across the street and facing down King street, where the town's people were assembled, and that the first rank was kneeling down, and the whole of the first platoon was presented, ready for firing on the word being given, and continued a considerable time in that posture, but by the providence of God they were restrained from firing.                                                    EBENEZER DORR.

Suffolk, ss.  Boston, March 21, 1770.  Ebenezer Dorr, above-named, after due examination, made oath to the truth of the aforesaid affidavit, taken to perpetuate the remembrance of the thing.

Before, JOHN RUDDOCK, Just. Peace and of the Quorum,
JOHN HILL, Just. Peace.

(No. 83.)

I, Edward Crafts, of lawful age, testify and say, that on Monday evening, the fifth instant, between 11 and 12 o'clock, Mr. Joseph Ayers met me at my gate, and I asked him where he was going. He answered, " To call Mr. Thomas Theodore Bliss to attend at the Council-chamber, to give evidence of the Captain's giving the soldiers orders to fire on the inhabitants." On leaving Mr. Bliss's door, there passed by us two corporals with about twenty soldiers, with muskets and fixed bayonets ; and on their observing our moving towards the Town-house, the soldiers halted, and surrounded us, saying we were a pack of damn'd rascals, and for three coppers they would blow our brains out. One of the corporals (viz. Eustice), gave orders for one-half the soldiers to cock, and the rest to make ready. On which we told them, we had nothing to say to them, but were on other business. The corporal, Eustice, struck Mr. Haldan, then in company, and turning to me, aimed a blow at my head with his firelock, which I took upon my arm, and then, with all his might, he made a pass at me, with his fixed bayonet, with full intent to take my life, as I thought. This I also parried with my naked hand. Then a soldier stepped out from among the rest, and presented his musket to my breast, and six or seven more at about eight or ten feet distance also presented. Upon this I called Corporal McCan, who came to me with a drawn sword or cutlass in his hand, and pushed the gun from my breast, saying, " This is Mr. Crafts, and if any of you offer to touch him again I will blow your brains out." Corporal Eustice answered and said, " He is as damn'd a rascal as any of them." The next evening about dusk coming by Rowe's barrack, I saw Corporal McCan who saved my life. He asked me if my arm was broke, I answered no. He said the gun with which Eustice struck me, was broke to pieces. And continued, " You would have been in heaven or hell in an instant if you had not called me by name. One man in particular, would have shot you, seven more presented at you !" He also said, his orders were, when the party came from the guard-house by the fortification, if any person or persons assaulted them, to fire upon them, every man being loaded with a brace of balls. And further I say not. EDWARD CRAFTS.

Suffolk, ss. Boston, March 17, 1770. Edward Crafts, above-named, after due examination, made oath to the truth of the above-written affidavit, taken to perpetuate the remembrance of the thing.

Before, RI. DANA, Just. of Peace and of the Quorum,
And, JOHN HILL, Just. Peace.

(No. 84.)

Joseph Allen, of lawful age, testifies and says, that between the hours of nine and ten on Monday evening the fifth instant, being at the dwelling-house of Mr. Winniet at New-Boston, was there informed that the town was alarmed by an affray between the soldiers and inhabitants; he immediately left said house, and after arming himself with a stout cudgel at Mr. Daniel Rea's, passed by Murray's barrack near Doctor Cooper's meeting-house, where were drawn up a party of soldiers with a number of officers in front ; and passing them quietly in company with Edward Winslow, Jun., was overtaken by a party of armed soldiers, one of whom laid hold of the deponent's neck of his coat and shirt, and tore the shirt, a second struck him over the shoulders, and either the latter or a third forcibly wrested the stick from him : Lieut. Minchin interposing prevented farther abuse, and entered into conversation with the deponent, complaining of the inhabitants for wrangling with the soldiers on the most trifling occasion. The deponent asked him if he thought a man could be inactive, when his countrymen were butchered in the street ? Lieut. Minchin answered, that " Mr. Mollineux was the author of all this." After the conversation was ended, or was nigh ending, Lieut. Minchin returned the deponent his stick ; and further saith not. JOSEPH ALLEN.

Suffolk, ss. Boston, March 16, 1770. Joseph Allen, above-named, after due examination, made oath to the truth of the above-written affidavit, taken to perpetuate the remembrance of the thing.

Before, RI. DANA, Just. of Peace and of the Quorum,
JOHN HILL, Just. Peace.

(No. 85.)

I, William Fallass, of lawful age, testify and say, that after the murder was committed in King street, on the evening of the fifth instant, upon my return home I had occasion to stop opposite to the lane leading to Green's barrack, and while I stood there the soldiers rushed by me with their arms, towards King street, saying, " This

is our time or chance ;" and that I never saw men or dogs so greedy
for their prey as these soldiers seemed to be, and the sergeants could
hardly keep them in their ranks.              WILLIAM FALLASS.
  Suffolk, ss.  Boston, March 16, 1770.  William Fallass, above-
      named, after due examination, made oath to the truth of
      the above-written affidavit, taken to perpetuate the remem-
      brance of the thing.
    Before, RI. DANA, Just. of Peace and of the Quorum,
      JOHN HILL, Just. Peace.

### (No. 86.)

  Mary Gardner, living in Atkinson street, of lawful age, testifies
and says, that on Monday evening the fifth day of March current,
and before the guns fired in King street, there were a number of soldiers assembled from Green's barrack towards the street and opposite her gate ; that they stood very still until the guns were fired in
King street, then they clapped their hands and gave a cheer, saying, " This is all that we want ;" they then ran to their barrack and
came out again in a few minutes, all with their arms, and ran towards King street.                          MARY GARDNER.
  Suffolk, ss.  Boston, March 20, 1770.  Mary Gardner, above-
      named, after due examination, made oath to the truth of
      the above-written affidavit, taken to perpetuate the remem-
      brance of the thing.
    Before, RI. DANA, Justice of Peace and of the Quorum,
      JOHN HILL, Justice Peace.

### (No. 87.)

  John Allman, of lawful age, testifies and says, that after the party
with the drum came from the main guard to Murray's barracks, he
saw the soldiers there drawn up under arms, and heard the officers,
as they walked backwards and forwards, say, " Damn it, what a fine
fire that was ! how bravely it dispersed the mob !"
                                            JOHN ALLMAN.
  Suffolk, ss.  Boston, March 16, 1770.  John Allman, above-named,
      after due examination, made oath to the truth of the above-
      written affidavit, taken to perpetuate the remembrance of
      the thing.
    Before, RI. DANA, Just. of Peace and of the Quorum,
      JOHN HILL, Just. Peace.

### (No. 88.)

  I, Benjamin Church, Jun., of lawful age, testify and say, that being
requested by Mr. Robert Pierpont, the Coroner, to assist in examining
the body of Crispus Attucks, who was supposed to be murdered by
the soldiers on Monday evening the 5th instant, I found two wounds
in the region of the thorax, the one on the right side, which entered
through the second true rib within an inch and a half of the sternum,

dividing the rib and separating the cartilaginous extremity from the sternum, the ball passed obliquely downward through the diaphragm and entering through the large lobe of the liver and the gall-bladder, still keeping its oblique direction, divided the aorta descendens just above its division into the iliacs, from thence it made its exit on the left side of the spine. This wound I apprehended was the immediate cause of his death. The other ball entered the fourth of the false ribs, about five inches from the linea alba, and descending obliquely passed through the second false rib, at the distance of about eight inches from the linea alba ; from the oblique direction of the wounds, I apprehend the gun must have been discharged from some elevation, and further the deponent saith not. BENJ. CHURCH, Jun.

Suffolk, ss. Boston, March 22, 1770. Benjamin Church, Jun., above-mentioned, after due examination, made oath to the truth of the aforesaid affidavit, taken to perpetuate the remembrance of the thing.

Before, JOHN RUDDOCK, Just. Peace and of the Quorum,
JOHN HILL, Just. Peace.

---

(No. 89.)

I, William Rhodes, of lawful age, testify and say, that on Tuesday March 6, 1770, the morning after the affair in King street, some of the seamen belonging to the Rose man-of-war, laying in the harbor of Boston, came to my shop, and after my asking them if they had heard of the affair that happened, they answered me " yes," and that all their boats were sent on shore manned, and that the master of the ship had kept them up all night, or the greatest part ; I then asked them whether they were kept to their quarters, they answered " no ;" I then asked whether they had loaded their guns, they likewise answered "no," but that they had been filling powder; some time after, I enquired of these same people whether their people when they came on shore on Monday night 5th March, were armed, they told me that the only person that had any arms was their master, who came ashore in the barge, and that he had only a pair of pistols, and that when they had got on the wharf that the said master gave the pistols to the coxswain of the barge ; and further saith not. WILLIAM RHODES.

Suffolk, ss. Boston, March 21, 1770. William Rhodes, above-named, after due examination, made oath to the truth of the aforesaid affidavit, taken to perpetuate the remembrance of the thing.

Before, JOHN RUDDOCK, Just. Peace and of the Quorum,
JOHN HILL, Just. Peace.

---

(No. 90.)

Mary Russell, of lawful age, declares that John Brailsford, a private soldier of the 14th regiment, who had frequently been employed by her (when he was ordered with his company to the castle, in consequence of the murders committed by the soldiers on the evening of

7

the 5th of Marcn), coming to the deponent's house, declared that
their regiment was ordered to hold themselves in readiness, and accordingly was ready that evening upon the inhabitants firing on the
soldiery to come to the assistance of the soldiery : on which the deponent asked him if he would have fired upon any of the inhabitants
of this town, to which he replied yes, if I had orders, but that if he
saw Mr. Russell he would have fired wide of him—he also said, " It's
well there was no gun fired by the inhabitants, for had there been, we
should have come to the soldiers' assistance." And further saith not.
                                                    MARY RUSSELL.
Suffolk, ss.  Boston, March 17, 1770.  The above-named Mary
        Russell, personally appearing, and being carefully examined,
        and duly cautioned to testify the whole truth, made solemn
        oath to the forewritten deposition by her subscribed.  Taken
        to perpetuate the remembrance of the thing.
    Before, JOHN RUDDOCK, Just. Peace and of the Quorum,
        JOHN HILL, Just. Peace.

---

(No. 91.)

I, Ephraim Fenno, of lawful age, testify, that on Friday the ninth
instant, as I was going home by the hospital in the common, I saw
Doctor Hall, surgeon of the 14th regiment, looking out of his window,
who said to me, " Dirty travelling, neighbor !"  " Yes, sir," returned
I.  He asked me what news in town ?  I told him I heard nothing
but what he already knew, that the talk was about the people that
were murdered.  He then asked me if the people of the town were
not easier ?  I replied, I believed not, nor would be till all the soldiers
had left the town.  He then asked me, if I heard whether the 14th
regiment was going ?  I answered yes, for the people would not be
quiet till they were all gone.  He said, the town's people had always
used the soldiers ill, which occasioned this affair, and said I wish that
instead of killing five or six, they had killed five hundred, damn me if
I don't.  And further I say not.                    EPHRAIM FENNO.
Suffolk, ss.  Boston, March 19, 1770.  Ephraim Fenno, above-
        named, after due examination, made oath to the truth of the
        aforesaid affidavit, taken to perpetuate the remembrance of
        the thing.
    Before, JOHN RUDDOCK, Just. Peace and of the Quorum,
        And, JOHN HILL, Just. Peace.

---

(No. 92.)

David Loring, who was much employed in making shoes for the
14th regiment, declares, that being at the woodyard of the 14th regiment on the 9th or 10th of March, talking with Serjeant Whittey, he
mentioned the unhappy affair of the murder committed by the soldiers
on the evening of the 5th instant, and said that he believed if the
14th regiment had been upon guard that day it would not have hap-

pened, and told him that he never liked the 29th regiment since they landed in Boston ; the serjeant asked the reason why he did not like the 29th regiment as well as the 14th ; he answered that they seemed to be a set of blood-thirsty men, and therefore did not like them, and believed the affair would have never happened had it not been for the affray of the 29th regiment at the rope-walks. A soldier of the 29th regiment named John Dudley being by, said it was a planned thing a month before. DAVID LORING.

Suffolk, ss. Boston, March 16, 1770. David Loring, above-named, after due examination, made oath to the truth of the aforesaid affidavit, taken to perpetuate the remembrance of the thing.

Before, JOHN RUDDOCK, Just. of Peace and of the Quorum,
JOHN HILL, Just. Peace.

---

(No. 93.)

I, the subscriber, being desired by the committee of inquiry to take ranges of the holes made by musket balls in two houses near opposite to the Custom-house, find that the bullet hole in the entry door post of Mr. Payne's house, and which grazed the edge of the door before it entered the post where it lodged, two and a half inches deep, ranges just under the stool of the western most lower chamber window of the Custom-house.

And that the hole made by another musket ball through the window shutter of the lower story of the same house, and lodged in the back wall of the shop, ranges about breast-high from the ground and between the second and third window from the west corner of the Custom-house.

And that the holes made in the shop of Warden and Vernon, through the outer shutter and back partition of the shop, ranged breast-high from the ground, and with the western most side of the first window west of the great door of the Custom-house.

BENJ. ANDREWS.

Suffolk, ss. Boston, March 20, 1770. Benjamin Andrews, Esq., above-named, after due examination, made oath to the truth of the aforesaid affidavit, taken to perpetuate the remembrance of the thing.

Before, JOHN RUDDOCK, Just. Peace and of the Quorum,
BELCHER NOYES, Just. Peace.

---

(No. 94.)

I, John Green, of lawful age, testify and say, that on Monday evening the 5th instant, just after nine o'clock, I went into the Custom-house, and saw in the kitchen of said house two boys belonging to Mr. Piemont the barber, and also my brother Hammond Green ; upon hearing an huzzaing and the bell ring, I went out, and there were but four or five boys in King street near the sentinel, who was muttering and growling, and seemed very mad. I saw Edward Gar-

rick who was crying, and told his fellow-apprentice that the sentinel
had struck him.  I then went as far as the Brazen-Head, and heard
the people huzzaing by Murray's barrack, I went down King-street
again, as far as the corner of Royal Exchange lane, by the sentry,
there being about forty or fifty people, chiefly boys, near the Custom-
house, but saw no person insult, or say anything to the sentry ; I then
said to Bartholomew Broaders, these words, viz. : the sentry (then
standing on the steps and loading his gun), is going to fire ; upon
which I went to the Custom-house gate and tried to get over the
gate, but could not ; whilst standing there, I saw Thomas Greenwood
upon the fence, to whom I said, open the gate ; he said that he would
not let his father in, and then jumped down into the lane and said to
the deponent, follow me ; upon which I went down the lane with him,
and round by the Post-office, to the main-guard ; he went into the
guard-house and said, turn out the guard, but the guard was out
before, and I heard that a party was gone to the Custom-house ; I
then heard the guns go off, one after another, and saw three persons
fall ; immediately after, a negro drummer beat to arms, upon that the
soldiers drew up in a rank (and I did not see Greenwood again, until
the next morning), after that I saw the 29th regiment drawn up in a
square, at the south-west corner of the Town-house ; soon after I went
home ; and further I say not.            JOHN GREEN.

  Suffolk, ss.   Boston, March 24, 1770.   John Green, above-
        named, after due examination, made oath to the truth of
        the above-written affidavit, taken to perpetuate the remem-
        brance of the thing.
  Before, JOHN RUDDOCK, Just. Peace and of the Quorum,
  And, JOHN HILL, Just. Peace.

### (No. 95.)

  I, Hammond Green, of lawful age, testify and say, that on the
evening of the 5th day of March instant, between the hours of eight and
nine o'clock, I went to the Custom-house ; when I came to the front
door of the said house, there were standing two young women
belonging to said house, and two boys belonging to Mr. Piemont, the
barber ; I went into the house and they all followed me, after that,
Mr. Sawny Irving came into the kitchen where we were, and afterwards I lighted him out at the front door, I then went back into the
kitchen again, and the boys above-mentioned went out ; after that,
two other boys belonging to Mr. Piemont, came into the kitchen, also
my brother John, who had been in a little while before, he went to the
back door and opened it, saying that something was the matter in the
street, upon which, with the other three, I went to the corner
of Royal Exchange-lane, in King-street, and heard an huzzaing, as I
thought, towards Dr. Cooper's meeting, and then saw one of the first-
mentioned boys, who said the sentry had struck him ; at which time,
there were not above eight or nine men and boys in King-street, after
that I went to the steps of the Custom-house door, and Mary Rogers,

Eliza Avery, and Ann Green, came to the door, at the same time, heard a bell ring; upon the people's crying fire, we all went into the house and I locked the door, saying, we shall know if anybody comes; after that, Thomas Greenwood came to the door and I let him in, he said that there was a number of people in the street, I told him if he wanted to see anything to go up stairs, but to take no candle with him; he went up stairs, and the three women aforementioned went with him, and I went and fastened the windows, doors, and gate; I left the light in the kitchen, and was going up stairs, but met Greenwood in the room next to the kitchen, and he said that he would not stay in the house, for he was afraid it would be pulled down, but I was not afraid of any such thing; I then went up stairs into the lower west chamber, next to Royal Exchange lane, and saw several guns fired in King-street, which killed three persons which I saw lay on the snow in the street, supposing the snow to be near a foot deep; after that, I let Eliza Avery out of the front door, and shut it after her, and went up chamber again; then my father, Mr. Bartholomew Green, came and knocked at the door, and I let him in; we both went into the kitchen and he asked me what was the matter, I told him that there were three persons shot by the soldiers who stood at the door of the Custom-house; he then asked me where the girls were, I told him they were up stairs, and we went up together, and he opened the window and I shut it again directly; he then opened it again and we both looked out; at which time Mr. Thomas Jackson, Jr., knocked at the door. I asked who was there. Mr. Jackson said, it is I, Hammond, let me in; I told him if my father was out, or any of the Commissioners came, I would not let them in. And further I say not.

HAMMOND GREEN.

Suffolk, ss. Boston, March 24, 1770. Hammond Green, above named, after due examination, made oath to the truth of the above-written affidavit, taken to perpetuate the remembrance of the thing.
Before, JOHN RUDDOCK, Just. Peace and of the Quorum,
JOHN HILL, Just. of Peace.

---

(No. 96.)

I, Thomas Greenwood, of lawful age, testify and say, that on Monday the 5th instant, spending the evening at Mrs. Wheeler's, I was alarmed by the bells ringing and people's crying fire, upon which I turned out with Mrs. Wheeler's three sons and helped Mr. Wheeler's engine as far as the Old South meeting-house, we met several people who told us it was not fire, but it was the soldiers and inhabitants fighting in King street, and desired them to go back and get their arms, upon hearing this, I hastened down to King street, and coming near the west door of the Town-house, I fell in with a number of people, most of them that I saw had sticks and clubs in their hands, and huzzaed, after that we went round the north side of the Town-house, and stood between the east steps of the Town-house and whipping-post; I

heard a number of people speaking, and one person in particular
spoke to the two sentinels, who were walking up and down the street
on the side of the Town-house, using these words,* "Come out and
fight us if you dare," calling them "Damned bloody back rascals and
scoundrels to come out and fight them, if they dared, we are enough
for you now," but I do not know whether the above person belonged
to the town; I looked round and saw about twenty people before the
Custom-house door, upon which I went down to the Custom-house, I
then heard two or three persons use these words, one after another,†
"I wish I could get into the Custom-house, I would make the money
circulate amongst us," after that I went up to the Custom-house door
and saw two or three snow-balls fall on the flat stones near the steps
of the door; I knocked and Mr. Hammond Green came to the door,
while I was speaking to the sentry, who stood upon the steps, I told
him not to let any body come into the door, and no person offered to
come in; the said Green asked who was there, I answered 'tis Thomas, let me in Hammond; when I got in, the said Green said to me if
I wanted to see anything, go up stairs, I went into the back room and
got the key of the little drawing-room, being the lower west corner
chamber, and went up stairs, and Elizabeth Avery, Mary Rogers and
Ann Green followed me into the room; we all looked through the
glass, I saw some persons standing by the sentry-box striking with
sticks, but did not see them hit any body, though a number of persons were close by them; I told the women above-mentioned that I
would not stay, for I was afraid that the house would be pulled down,
there being about forty or fifty persons consisting of men and boys;
I saw no persons throw any stones or attempt to break even a square
of glass, or get into the house (the next morning I found there was
not a pane of glass broke in the said house). Afterwards, I went down
stairs and met Hammond Green in the middle room; he asked me
where I was going, I told him I was going out, upon which I went
into the kitchen and took my hat and went into the yard, got upon the
wood pile and went to the fence; John Green being by the gate

* It may not be improper to remark here, that the deponent, Thomas Greenwood, is a hired servant to the Commissioners, on whom he is altogether dependent, and when before the Justices, he was several times detected in plain
falsehoods; particularly in swearing first, that the number of persons who
called the soldiers "bloody back rascals," &c., was nine, then seven, and
finally but one, as it now stands; and through the whole of his examination
he was so inconsistent and so frequently contradicted himself, that all present were convinced no credit ought to be given to his deposition, for which
reason it would not have been inserted had it not been known that a deposition was taken relating to this affair, from this Greenwood, by Justice Murray, and carried home by Mr. Robinson.
† As this deponent is the only person out of a great number of witnesses
examined, who heard any mention made of the Custom-house, and as it is
very uncommon for several people to repeat exactly the same words upon
such occasions (for the deponent insisted that the identical words were used by
each person) considering the character and connections of the deponent, and
his own express declaration in this affidavit, that he saw no person attempt
even to break a square of glass or to get into the Custom-house, it may very
justly be doubted whether such words were used by any one.

asked me to open the gate and let him in ; I told him I would not open the gate for any body ; one person passing by, said to me, heave over some shillelahs. I jumped off the fence into Royal Exchange lane, went down the lane with John Green, and went round by the post-office to the main-guard ; I told one of the soldiers if they did not go down to the sentry at the Custom-house,* I was afraid they would hurt him, though I had not seen any person insult him, some body said they were gone ; I stood with John Green near the guard-house, saw the guns go off and heard the report; afterwards I heard a person say, which I took to be a soldier, "That's right, damn them, kill them all, they have no business there," and from thence I went to the house of Mr. Burch, one of the Commissioners, where I saw Mr. Burch and wife, Mr. Paxton, another Commissioner, and Mr. Reeves, Secretary to the Board ; one of the Commissioners asked me what was the matter, I told him the soldiers had fired upon the inhabitants, and had killed two or three, and wounded some more, upon which Mr. Reeves said, " God bless my soul," and then went into the other room. I left Mr. Burch's house and went to the barracks at Wheelwright's Wharf, and staid there all night ; I heard several soldiers say, " They wished they were let out, for if they were, there should not be many people alive in the morning ;" the whole of the 14th regiment being under arms, and the piquet guard went to the main guard-house about 12 o'clock that night.                           THOMAS GREENWOOD.

Suffolk, ss.   Boston, March 24, 1770.   Thomas Greenwood, above-
          named, after due examination, made oath to the truth of the
          above-written affidavit, taken to perpetuate the remembrance
          of the thing.
     Before, JOHN RUDDOCK, Just. Peace and of the Quorum,
     And, JOHN HILL, Just. Peace.

                                         BOSTON, the 22d March, 1770.
     We, the subscribers, two of his Majesty's Justices of the Peace for the County of Suffolk (one being of the Quorum) hereby certify, that Col. William Dalrymple, chief commander of the soldiers in Boston, William Sheaffe, Esq., deputy collector of the customs, and Bartholomew Green, head of the family in the Custom-house in Boston, were duly notified to attend the captions of the affidavits *in perpetuam*, &c., touching the massacre by the soldiers in Boston, taken before us on the 16th, 17th, and 19th days of March current ; and that the said William Sheaffe and Bartholomew Green attended accordingly, on the 16th of March, and cross-examined as many of the deponents as they thought fit and as long as they pleased, but declined giving any further attendance.                           RI. DANA,
                                                             JOHN HILL.

     * It seems very difficult, according to Greenwood's account, to form even a conjecture of the reason of his fears, which he expressed for the sentry, when in the same breath he declares that he had not seen any person insult him. But probably the true motives of his application to the main-guard were not of a nature to be made public.

SUFFOLK, SS.                              *Boston, March* 30, 1770.

We do hereby certify, that the several copies contained in the annexed printed collection of affidavits, taken before us *in perpetuam,* &c., have been carefully compared by us with the originals, and agree therewith.

> RI. DANA, Justice of Peace, and of the Quorum.
> JOHN HILL, Justice of Peace.

We do certify the like, respecting those affidavits taken before us.

> RI. DANA, Justice of Peace, and of the Quorum.
> SAM. PEMBERTON, Justice of Peace.

We do certify the like, respecting the affidavit taken before us.

> RI. DANA, Justice of Peace, and of the Quorum.
> JOHN RUDDOCK, Justice of Peace, and of the Quorum.

We do certify the like, respecting the affidavit taken before us.

> RI. DANA, Justice of Peace, and of the Quorum.
> JOHN TUDOR, Justice of the Peace.

We do certify the like, respecting those affidavits taken before us.

> JOHN RUDDOCK, Justice of Peace, and of the Quorum.
> JOHN HILL, Justice of Peace.

We do certify the like, respecting those affidavits taken before us.

> JOHN RUDDOCK, Justice of Peace and of the Quorum.
> BELCHER NOYES, Justice of Peace.

We do certify the like, respecting the affidavit taken before us.

> JOHN RUDDOCK, Justice of Peace, and of the Quorum.
> JOHN TUDOR, Justice of Peace.

I do hereby certify, that the copy of an affidavit (contained in the annexed printed collection of affidavits,) taken before me, has been carefully compared by me with the original, and agrees therewith.

> EDM. QUINCY, J. Pacis.

————————◆◀◉▶◆————————

[SEAL]

T. HUTCHINSON.

By the Honorable THOMAS HUTCHINSON, Esq., Lieutenant Governor and Commander-in-Chief, in and over his Majesty's Province of Massachusetts Bay in New England.

I do hereby certify that Richard Dana and John Ruddock, Esquires, are two of his Majesty's Justices of the Peace and of the Quorum for the County of Suffolk, within the aforesaid Province ; and that John Hill, Edmund Quincy, Belcher Noyes, John Tudor, and Samuel Pemberton, Esquires, are Justices of the Peace for the same County, and that full faith and credit is and ought to be given to their several acts and attestations (as on the annexed paper) both in Court and without.

In testimony whereof I have caused the Public Seal of the Province of Massachusetts Bay abovesaid to be hitherto affixed. Dated at Boston the thirteenth day of March, 1770. In the tenth year of his Majesty's reign.

By his Honor's Command,
JOHN COTTON, D. Sec'ry.

---

☞ Three original certificates of the foregoing tenor, with the Province Seal affixed to them, are signed by the Lieutenant Governor, and annexed to three printed copies of this pamphlet.

Two of them will be sent to London for the satisfaction of such gentlemen in England as incline to see the originals : viz, one of them to WILLIAM BOLLAN, Esq., and the other to DENNIS DEBERTDT, Esq.— The third remains with the Committee.

———•●•———

In pursuance of a vote of the Town of the 22d of March, the Committee sent printed copies of the foregoing Pamphlet, accompanied with letters, to his Royal Highness the Duke of GLOUCESTER, his Royal Highness the Duke of Cumberland, and also to the Lords and other persons of character, whose titles and names follow,* viz.,

His Grace the Duke of RICHMOND,
Duke of GRAFTON.
The Right Honorable the Lord CAMDEN.
The Most Noble the Marquis of ROCKINGHAM.
The Rt. Hon. the Earl of ROCHFORD.
Earl of HALIFAX.
Earl of DARTMOUTH.
Earl TEMPLE.
Earl of NORTHINGTON.
Earl of CHATHAM.
Earl of HILLSBOROUGH.
Earl of SHELBURNE.
Lord Viscount WEYMOUTH.
Lord MANSFIELD.
Lord LYTTLETON.
*Peers of the Realm.*

* This list and the following letter are annexed to such copies only of this pamphlet as are intended for publication in America.

Sir JOHN CUST, Speaker of the House of Commons.
Sir FLETCHER NORTON, the succeeding Speaker.
The Marquis of GRANBY.
Sir EDWARD HAWKE.
Sir GEORGE SAVILLE.
GEORGE GRENVILLE, Esq.
WILLIAM DOWDESWELL, Esq.
WILLIAM BECKFORD, Esq., Lord Mayor of LONDON.
The Honorable Sir WILLIAM MEREDITH.
ALEX. MACKAY, Esq., Col. of the 64th Regiment.
RICHARD JACKSON, Esq.
JOHN WILKES, Esq., ⎫
JOHN GLYNN, Esq., ⎬ Knights of the Shire for MIDDLESEX.
EDMUND BURKE, Esq.
JAMES TOWNSHEND, Esq.
JOHN LAWBRIDGE, Esq.
THOMAS WHATELY, Esq.
ALEXANDER WEDDERBURN, Esq.
                    *Members of the Honorable House of Commons.*

The Right Honorable Sir JOHN EARLDLY WILMOT.
The Society for the Support of Magna Charta, and the Bill of
    Rights.
THOMAS HOLLIS, Esq., F. R. S.
Mrs. CATHERINE MACAULAY.
JOHN POMEROY, Esq., Col. of the 65th Regiment, and a Member
    of Parliament in Ireland.
Doctor CHARLES LUCAS, Member of Parliament in Ireland.

The Committee sent like copies, and also writ, to the Gentlemen
mentioned in the Town vote prefixed to the foregoing Narrative.

The following is a copy of the Letter wrote by the Committee to
the Duke of Richmond ; to which [excepting the last paragraph of
it] the other letters, *mutatis mutandis,* correspond.

To his Grace the Duke of Richmond.
                    Boston, New England, March 23, 1770.
MY LORD DUKE,

It is in consequence of the appointment of the Town of Boston,
that we have the honor of writing to your Grace, and of communi-
cating the enclosed Narrative, relating to the Massacre in this Town
on the 5th instant.

After that execrable deed, perpetrated by soldiers of the 29th
Regiment, the town thought it highly expedient that a full and just
representation of it should be made to persons of character, in order to
frustrate the designs of certain men, who, as they have heretofore
been plotting the ruin of our constitution and liberties, by their
letters, memorials, and representations, are now said to have procured
depositions in a private manner, relative to the said Massacre, to bring
an odium upon the Town, as the aggressors in that affair : But we

humbly apprehend, your Grace, after examining the said Narrative and the depositions annexed to it, will be fully satisfied of the falsehood of such a suggestion; and we take upon ourselves to declare upon our honor and consciences, that having examined critically into the matter, there does not appear the least ground for it.

The depositions referred to (if any such there be) were taken without notifying the Select Men of the Town or any other persons whatever, to be present at the caption, in behalf of the Town : of which conduct as it has been justly complained of heretofore in other cases, so the Town now renew their complaint in the present case; and humbly presume such depositions will have no weight, till the Town has been served with copies of them, and an opportunity given the Town to be heard in their defence, in this matter ; and in any other, wherein their character is drawn into question, with a view of passing a censure upon it.

A different conduct was observed on the part of the Town. The Justices with a committee to assist them, made their examinations publicly ; most of them at Faneuil Hall, and the rest where any person might attend. Notifications were sent to the Custom-house, where the Commissioners of the Customs sit, that they or any persons in their behalf, might be present at the captions : Accordingly Mr. Sheafe the deputy collector, and Mr. Green, tenant of the Custom-house under the Commissioners, and employed by them, were present at many of them.*

One of the said Commissioners, Mr. Robinson, in a secret manner has embarked on board Capt. Robson, and sailed for London the 16th instant, which, with three of the other Commissioners retiring from the Town, and not having held a board for some time since the 5th instant,† gives reason to apprehend, they have planned, and are executing a scheme of misrepresentation, to induce administration to think, that their persons are not in safety in this Town, in the absence of the Troops. But, my Lord, their safety is in no wise dependent on Troops ; for your Grace must be sensible, that if any evil had ever been intended them, Troops could not have prevented it.

It was so apparently incompatible with the safety of the Town, for the Troops to continue any longer in it, that his Majesty's Council were unanimous in their advice to the Lieutenant-Governor, that they should be removed to the barracks at Castle Island. And it is the humble and fervent prayer of the Town and the Province in general, that his Majesty will graciously be pleased, in his great wisdom and goodness, to order the said Troops out of the Province; and that his dutiful and loyal subjects of this Town and Province—dutiful and loyal notwithstanding any representations to the contrary—may not again be distressed and destroyed by Troops; for preventing which we beg leave in behalf of the Town, to request most earnestly the favor of your Interposition and Influence.

* See the Deposition of the Justices, page 103.

† No Board has been held from the 9th of March, to the time of printing this Letter, viz., May 16th, and it is uncertain when there will be one.

The candor and justice of your Grace, so conspicuous in the last Session of Parliament, when your Grace was pleased to move in the House of Lords, that the Resolves then under consideration, and afterwards passed by that right honorable House, for censuring this Town and Province, should be suspended, till we could have opportunity of being heard on the subject of them,—the candor and justice so conspicuous in that motion will always endear to us the personage that made it. And they give us the strongest Reason to hope for your Patronage, in everything not inconsistent with those virtues. We have the honor to be, with the most perfect regard,

My Lord Duke,

Your Grace's most obedient

and very humble Servants,

JAMES BOWDOIN.

SAMUEL PEMBERTON.

JOSEPH WARREN.

# ADDITIONAL OBSERVATIONS

TO

# A SHORT NARRATIVE

OF THE

## HORRID MASSACRE IN BOSTON,

PERPETRATED

## IN THE EVENING OF THE 5TH OF MARCH, 1770.

---

PRINTED BY ORDER OF THE TOWN OF BOSTON, MDCCLXX.

·

# ADDITIONAL OBSERVATIONS.

THE extraordinary conduct of the Commissioners of the Customs since the 5th of March, and their perseverance in it, make it necessary to bestow a few observations upon it; and upon divers matters, with which it seems to be connected.*

The said Commissioners (excepting Mr. Temple) have all retired from the town : and we find, on particular enquiry, they have not held a meeting of their Board since the 9th of March. How they have disposed of themselves since that time we shall here relate.

Mr. Robinson is gone to England. He sailed the 16th of March, and went not only without the leave, but, as it is said, contrary to the minds of his superiors, signified to him from home. None but the few, intrusted with the secret, knew anything of his going till after the departure of the vessel in which he went.

Mr. Paxton retired to Cambridge, four miles from Boston, and for the most part has continued there. He has divers times, however, visited the town since that retiring.

Mr. Hulton sometime ago purchased a place at Brooklyn, five miles from Boston, and has ever since resided there.

Mr. Burch, with his wife, has retired to Mr. Hulton's, who, together with Mr.. Burch (leaving their wives behind them) are now on a tour to Portsmouth, in the province of New Hampshire, where the last account from thence left them. It is now above six weeks since a Board of Commissioners was held : and it is utterly uncertain when there will be another.

From their first establishment here, to the 11th of June, 1768, they

---

* The copies of this Narrative, sent to England and other parts, conclude with the foregoing pages. Since they were sent, it has appeared necessary to add a few pages to the remaining copies : to do which an opportunity has been given by the restraint laid on the publishing of said narrative here. The reason of that restraint will appear by the following vote of the Town, passed at the Town-Meeting held the 26th of March, namely : " The Committee appointed to prepare the true state of facts, relating to the execrable Massacre perpetrated on the evening of the 5th instant, in order that the same be transmitted to Great Britain, having accordingly reported, and the Report being accepted by the Town and ordered to be printed : And whereas the publishing of the said Narrative with the Depositions accompanying it, in this county, may be supposed by the unhappy persons now in custody for trial, as tending to give an undue bias to the minds of the Jury, who are to try the same : Therefore, voted, That the Committee reserve all the printed copies in their hands, excepting those to be sent to Great Britain, till the further order of the Town.

"Attest,    WILLIAM COOPER, Town-Clerk."

held their Boards regularly four days every week. They then retired on board the *Romney* man-of-war, and from thence to the Castle: for what purpose, their letters and memorials lately published have sufficiently informed the world. From their re-establishment in Boston in November, 1768, to the 5th of March, 1770, they held their Boards in the same regular manner. Since that time there have been but two Board meetings, the last of which was on the 9th of March.

Now what do all these manœuvres since the 5th of March indicate? Is it possible to suppose they indicate anything less than a design to take occasion from the outrages and murders committed on the evening of that day by the soldiers (assisted perhaps from the Custom-house) to represent the town in a disadvantageous light? And does not their former conduct render this highly probable? Besides, it is a fact, that Depositions have been taken in a secret manner, relative to that unhappy affair, to the prejudice of the town; and it is no way improbable that Mr. Robinson is gone home with memorials and letters from the Commissioners and others, accompanying such depositions.

By some escapes, as well as by what the circumstances above-mentioned make probable, a pretty good judgment may be formed of the substance of those memorials, letters, and depositions, namely, that the Custom-house was attacked—the revenue chest in danger, but saved by the firing upon the *mob*—the King's troops compelled to leave the town—the Commissioners thence obliged for their safety to quit it also—the consequent impossibility of their holding Boards —the detriment thence arising to the revenue and his Majesty's service —all government at an end, and the Province in a state of rebellion.

If these be, either in whole or in part, the subject of the dispatches sent home, it is very proper a few observations should be made upon them.

The Custom-house attacked—a falsehood. The people drawn into King street, were drawn thither by the cry of fire, and the outrages of the soldiers, which occasioned it. From the first appearance of the people in King street, to the time of the firing upon them, there had not passed fifteen minutes. It might with as much truth be affirmed, that they made an attack upon the Custom-house in London, as upon the Custom-house in Boston: of which latter there was not even a pane of glass broken.

The revenue chest in danger—a falsehood. It is not probable the chest is kept at the Custom-house; but if it be, there was, and is, at least as much danger of it from some of the out-door people employed under the Commissioners, as from any body else. It is certain that some of them are of an infamous character.

The troops compelled to quit the town—a falsehood. They quitted the town by the orders of their commanding officer, in consequence of a request from the Lieutenant Governor, who was advised by the council to pray the said officer to remove the troops. This request and this prayer was obtained by an application from the town to the Lieutenant Governor. Into what times are we fallen, that the government of the province is reduced to the humiliating condition of making such a prayer!

But supposing the troops had been compelled *vi et armis* to quit the town. It would have been a measure justifiable in the sight of God and man. When the soldiers, sent hither for the declared purpose of assisting the civil magistrate to keep the peace, were themselves in a remarkable manner the breakers of the peace—when, instead of assisting, they insulted him ; and rescued offenders of their own corps from justice—when they frequently abused the inhabitants in the night—when they had entered into a combination to commit some extraordinary acts of violence upon the town ; and in consequence of it, on the evening of the massacre, attacked the inhabitants wherever they met them; afterwards firing upon, and killing and wounding a number of them—when all this had been done, and more threatened, it was high time they should be removed from the town. If there had been no other means of getting rid of them, the inhabitants would have had a right by that law of nature, which supersedes all other laws, when they come in competition with it—the law of self-preservation—to have compelled them to quit the town. This law is radical in our nature, indelible from it, and uniformly operating where it can operate, to the removal or destruction of every thing incompatible with it; and is abrogable by no other law-giver than God himself, the great author of it. Therefore, although the resisting the King's troops in any thing they have a right by law to do, may be adjudged treason, yet when they act contrary to law, especially in so outrageous a manner as in the present case, and retain a disposition to repeat it, whereby the lives of the King's subjects are in danger, they then cease to be the King's troops; that is, they are not the King's troops for any such purpose, but so far become traitors ; and on the failure of other means of riddance from them, which the time and circumstances may make eligible and are lawful, they may (by the principles of all law, as well as by the great law above-mentioned, into which those principles are resolvable) be resisted and expelled ; and not to do it, where it can be done, is a species of treason against the constitution, and consequently treason in an equal degree against the King and all his subjects.

The Commissioners obliged for their safety to quit the town.—If one falsehood can be more so than another, this is the greatest yet mentioned, and is as ridiculous as it is false. Their conduct and such a declaration by no means agree. Would they in that case occasionally visit the town ? Would they trust themselves in the environs of it ? Could they think themselves safe at Cambridge and Brookline ? Could they think themselves safe anywhere in the province, or indeed in America ? Must they not know, if any evil were really intended them, it might easily overtake them any where, and every where on this side of the Atlantic ? Some other reason than their safety must therefore be looked for to account for their retiring, and discontinuing their boards. A similar proceeding of theirs in June, 1768, and their letters and memorials lately published, give occasion at least to conjecture what that reason may be. Is it not probable it was to corroborate the said

8

depositions, and thence induce administration to think it necessary, not only that the troops already here should be continued, but that a further number should be sent to strengthen and support them ?  If this measure cannot be effected, and should the Commissioners be so un-fortunate as to remain here unattacked in the absence of the troops, it might naturally be thought they could have remained here without them in 1768 ; and therefore that they had put the nation to a very great expense, for no other purpose than further to alienate the affections of the Americans, and to give them an additional reason to wish themselves independent of it.  And hence the Commissioners might have cause to expect a national resentment against them.  However injurious to us the effects of such policy may be, we cannot but applaud it (on the principles of the Machiavelian system) as it stands related to themselves.  If they thought their own existence in danger, considered as Commissioners, how natural was it to use the means to support it ? And what fault could be found with the means, if those principles justified them ?  Why need they trouble their heads about consequences that would not affect themselves ?  or, if they would, and such existence appeared precarious without those means, was it not necessary they should be used, and the consequences disregarded ?  If the means be successful to the end for which they seemed designed, it requires no prophetic spirit to foretell that the consequences may be —— bad enough.  Whether the present Commissioners, or any board of Commissioners at all (whose appointments are fully equal to any benefit the nation or colonies are like to reap from them, and whose usefulness hitherto may be valued by some of the negative quantities in algebra) are things of importance enough to hazard those consequences, or any ill consequence at all, is humbly submitted to the wisdom of administration to determine.

The consequent impossibility of their holding boards.—This impossibility was of their own creating.  If they had continued in town (from whence they had not the least reason to depart, unless to answer purposes they would choose to conceal) they might have held their boards as usual.

The detriment thence raising to the Revenue, and his Majesty's service.—If any such detriment has arisen, the fault is their own. *His Majesty's service*, is a cant term in the mouths of understrappers in office.  Many of them either do not know the meaning of it, or abuse it to answer their own corrupt purposes.  It is used to express something distinct from the service of the people.  The king and people are placed by it in opposite interests.  Whereas, by the happy constitution we are under, the interest of the King is the interest of the people, and his service is their service : both are one, and constitutionally inseparable.  They who attempt to separate them, attempt to destroy the constitution.  Upon every such parricide may the vengeance both of King and People descend.

Government at an end.—This has been the cry ever since the Stamp-Act existed.  If the people saw they were going to be enslaved ; if they saw Governor Bernard (from whom they had a right to expect that he would do nothing to promote it) was zealous and active to rivet the chains; and that his government, in its principles and conduct, tended to the establishment of a tyranny over them, was it unnatural for them in such a case to reluct? was it unreasonable to refuse an acquiescence in such measures? Did an opposition to them indicate a disregard to government? If government, in the true idea of it, has for its object the good of the governed, *such* an administration could not be called government: and an opposition to it by no means included an opposition to government. From such an opposition has arisen the cry, that government is at an end. The sooner *such* government is at an end the better.

When a people have lost all confidence in government, it is vain to expect a cordial obedience to it. Hence irregularities may arise, and have arisen. But they will cease, when the true ends of government are steadily pursued. Then, and not till then, may it be expected, that men of weight and influence will exert themselves to make government respected. Nay, such exertions will then be needless, for mankind cannot help respecting what is in itself respectable, especially when it is at the same time so promotive of their own good as good government is.

The province in a state of rebellion.—Into this state its enemies, on both sides of the *Atlantic*, have been endeavoring to bring it. When they could not make it subservient to their interest and views; and when their measures had raised a spirit of opposition to them, that opposition was made the lucky occasion to represent the province in a state of rebellion, or verging towards it. To justify such a representation the more fully, they endeavored to drive it into that state: whereby in the end they might hope to gratify both their malice and avarice; their malice by injuring it most essentially; and their avarice, by the subjection of it to their tyranny and pillage. But nothing can be more false than such a representation: nothing more foreign from this people than a disposition to rebellion. The principles of loyalty were planted in our breasts too deep to be eradicated by *their* efforts, or any efforts whatever; and our interest co-operated with those principles.

It is humbly hoped his Majesty will not be influenced by *such* representations to think unfavorably of *his faithful subjects of this province:* and *that* hope is grounded upon their innocence: of which they have the highest evidence in their own consciousness; and of which they have given their adversaries no other cause to doubt, than what arises from an opposition to *their* measures. Measures, not only ruinous to the province, but hurtful to *Great Britain,* and destructive of the union, and commercial intercourse, which ought always to subsist between her and her Colonies.

The foregoing Observations appeared necessary to vindicate the Town and Province from the aspersions so unjustly cast upon them. The few that follow refer to the present and future state of *Great Britain* and her Colonies:

How happy is *Britain* with regard to situation and many internal circumstances; and in her connection with her Colonies!

Separated from the rest of the world, and possessed of so large a naval force, she is secure from foreign invasions : her government (well administered) is the best existing; her manufactures are extensive, and her commerce in proportion.   To the two latter the Colonies have in a considerable degree contributed.   By these means she has risen to her present opulence and greatness, which so much distinguish her among the powers of *Europe*.   But however great and opulent she may be, she is capable of being still more so ; and so much so, that she may be deemed at present in a state of minority, compared with what she will one day probably be, if her own conduct does not prevent it.   The means of this greatness are held out to her by the Colonies ; and it is in her power, by a kind and just treatment of them, to avail herself of those means.

The Colonists are husbandmen, and till lately have manufactured but a small part of their clothing, and the other articles with which they had been usually supplied from *Great Britain*.   But they have been taught by experience they can supply themselves; and that experience (which has been forced upon them) has demonstrated most clearly, that they have within themselves the means of living conveniently, if not with elegance, even if their communication with the rest of mankind were wholly cut off.   This, however, could not be an eligible state : but no one entitled to and deserving the liberties of an Englishman, can hesitate a moment to say, that it would be preferable to slavery ; to which the Colonists have apprehended themselves doomed, by the measures that have been pursued by Administration.   If the Colonists might be permitted to follow their inclinations, with which at the same time their interest coincides, they would be husbandmen still, and be supplied as usual from Great Britain.   The yearly amount of those supplies (as appears by the exports from Britain) is very considerable,* and might be in future in proportion to the increase of the Colonists.

* The value of the exports from Britain to the Colonies in 1766, which was less than in 1765, stood thus :—

| | |
|---|---:|
| To New England, . . . . | £409,642 |
| New York, . . . . . | 330,829 |
| Pennsylvania, . . . . | 327,314 |
| Virginia and Maryland, . . . | 372,548 |
| Carolina, . . . . . | 296,732 |
| | £1,737,065 |

This is taken from "The present state of the Nation," in which there is an account of the said exports for the years 1765 and 1766 only.

Now supposing the observation just, that the Colonists (whose number by the said Pamphlet is estimated two millions) double every twenty years, and the exports from Great Britain to the Colonies should increase in that proportion, the value of the said exports and the number of the Colonists, at the end of five such periods after 1766, will stand thus :—

VALUE OF EXPORTS.

In 1766  £1,737,065 for two millions of Colonists.
    1786   3,474,130 for four millions.
    1806   6,948,260 for eight millions.
    1826  13,896,520 for sixteen millions.

Their increase is rapid : they are daily emigrating from the old towns, and forming new ones : and if they double their numbers every twenty years, as it is said they will continue to do, so long as they can form into families by procuring the means of subsistence at an easy rate, which probably will be the case till America shall be well peopled, there will be in a short time a prodigious addition to his Majesty's subjects ; who if not compelled to manufacture for themselves, will occasion a proportionable demand for the manufactures of Great Britain. If it be considered, too, that America, from its different soils and climates, can raise perhaps all the productions of other countries in the same latitudes ; which being remitted in exchange would most of them be rough materials for Britain to manufacture ; what a fund of wealth and power will America be to her ! Her inhabitants, of every denomination, by finding employment, and the consequent means of subsistence, will greatly increase ; and her trade and navigation be in proportion. She might then view with indifference the interdiction of her trade with other parts of the world ; though she would always have it in her power, from the superiority of her naval force, which such a trade and navigation would enable her to support, to do herself justice, and command universal respect.

Connected with her Colonies, she would then be a mighty empire : the greatest, consisting of people of one language, that ever existed.

If these observations be not wholly visionary, and a mere reverie, they possibly may not be unworthy the consideration of Parliament : whose wisdom will determine, whether any revenue whatever, even the greatest that America could possibly produce, either without or with her good will, would compensate the loss of such wealth and power ; or justify measures that had the least tendency to bring them into hazard : or whether for such a revenue it would be worth while to hazard even the present advantages, resulting to Great Britain from an union and harmony with her Colonies.

In 1846 $27,793,040 for thirty-two millions.
1866    55,586,080 for sixty-four millions of Colonists.

The last mentioned numbers are so large, that it is likely the principles on which they are formed may be called into question. Let us therefore take only one-quarter part of those numbers, and then the value of exports from Britain to the Colonies, in 1866, will be more than thirteen millions sterling for sixteen millions of Colonists. It is highly probable, by that time there will be at least that number of Colonists in the British Colonies on this continent. Now, in case there be no interruption of the union and harmony that ought to subsist between Great Britain and her Colonies, and which it is their mutual interest should subsist and be maintained, what good reason can be given why such exports should not bear as great a proportion to the number of the Colonists as they do at this time ? If they should, the value of such exports (which will be continually increasing) will be at least thirteen millions per annum. A sum far surpassing the value of all the exports from Great Britain at this day.

In what proportion so vast a trade with the Colonies would enlarge the other branches of her trade ; how much it would increase the number of her people, the rents and value of her lands, her wealth of every species, her internal strength, her naval power, and particularly her revenue (to enhance which in a trifling degree has occasioned the present uneasiness between her and the Colonies) are matters left to the calculation and decision of the political arithmeticians of Great Britain.

AN

# INDEX TO THE APPENDIX.

---

## L.

## M.

## N.

## P.

## R.

## S.

## T.